COMPUTER AIDED
FLAT SKETCHING
for the
FASHION INDUSTRY

COMPUTER AIDED

FLAT SKETCHING

for the

FASHION INDUSTRY

Barbara Sultan

Born in New York City Barbara Sultan has had extensive experience as a clothing designer. Sultan has been painting and drawing using the computer as a tool for the past 18 years, using numerous drawing programs.

A strong creative vision along with a commitment to detail and quality have been hallmarks to Sultan's 20 year career as a fashion designer , both in New York City and Los Angeles.

Sultan has been teaching at the Fashion Institute of Design and Merchandising in Los Angeles for 19 years. Where she currently teaches drawing in the design and manufacturing programs. Sultan is the designer and owner of Da' Max design and publications and Da-Max.com. Sultan lectures at various universities on fashion design, art, and the computer.

Other books by Sultan:
Flat Sketching for the Fashion Industry
Applied Flat Sketching for the Fashion Industry

Library of Congress Cataloging-in-Publication Data

ISBN 0-9647196-7-3

Printed in the United States of America

Published by Da' Max
P.O. Box 50575
Los Angeles, California 90050
www. Da-Max.com

INTRODUCTION

This book is a creative approach to drawing garments using specific tools from the Adobe Illustrator program. It introduces the general concepts of computer-aided **FLAT SKETCHING DESIGN.** The worksheets provide a highly visual starting point for understanding the **CAD** system in relationship to **FASHION DESIGN.** This is a step-by-step method with a useful library of technical data. Readers can expect to develop a working knowledge of the software as a useful tool for students and professionals. This text assumes you have basic experience with the computer; including how to use a mouse, standard menus, and opening and saving files.

In the fashion business, it is important to communicate your designs with a working sketch. Using this program, you will develop the skill of drawing a flat sketch with accurate proportion and detail.

To create effective flats you need to understand some basic concepts. Computer design falls into two main catagories........vector graphics and bitmap imaging. The difference is smooth lines versus pixilated lines. Understanding the difference between the two helps you to create and edit your work. This is as much as I will say about vector versus bitmap programs. You can read more about this in your Adobe Illustrator book under "vector".

Special thanks to :

George Chialtas...................illustrations & photography

Sunyoung Chung................illustrations

Lori Lane.................................fashion update & graphics

Jacqui Wou-Ross ....editing & cover

Martin Sultan........................editing & support

"I STAND ON THE SHOULDERS OF GIANTS"

TABLE OF CONTENTS

GETTING STARTED

WOMEN'S WEAR

TABLE OF CONTENTS

WOMEN'S WEAR

TABLE OF CONTENTS

INFANTS / KIDS WEAR

TABLE OF CONTENTS

MENSWEAR

GETTING
STARTED

GETTING STARTED W/ TERMINOLOGY of TOOLS

THESE ARE THE SELECTED TOOLS THAT ARE USED IN THIS BOOK TO CREATE FLAT SKETCHES. YOU WILL BE GUIDED THROUGH OUT THIS BOOK HOW TO USE THESE TOOLS.

 SELECTION TOOL.......SELECTS ENTIRE OBJECTS SUCH AS A WHOLE GARMENT, ALL THE PIECES.

 DIRECT SELECTION TOOL......SELECTS A PORTION OF A SLEEVE, COLLAR OR INDIVIDUAL LINES AND ANCHOR POINTS.

POP OUT MENU

ANCHOR POINT EDITING TOOLS ARE UNDER PEN TOOL.

 PEN TOOL..........CREATES LINES AND SMOOTH CURVES. THE MOST POWERFUL DRAWING TOOL. GREAT ACCURACY FOR DRAWING GARMENTS.

 ELLIPSE TOOL.........VERY GOOD FOR BUTTON SHAPES AND LOGOS.

 RECTANGLE TOOL.......MAKES GREAT POCKETS AND FRAMES.

 REFLECT TOOL...NEEDED TO FLIP 1/2 A GARMENT TO MAKE A COMPLETE GARMENT W/ACCURACY.

ADD ANCHOR POINT TOOL

 ROTATE TOOL........POSITIONS AN OBJECT AT ANY ANGLE THAT YOU WANT.

 TYPING TOOL..........CREATES AND EDITS TYPE.

DELETE ANCHOR POINT TOOL

 EYE DROPPER TOOL.........PICKS UP SAMPLES OF PAINT USED IN FILLING A GARMENT.

 ZOOM TOOL.......MAGNIFIES OR REDUCES THE VIEW OF ANY OBJECT. GOES REAL FAST.

CONVERT TOOL

 SCALE TOOL........REDUCES OR ENLARGES GARMENTS.

GETTING STARTED W/ FILL AND STROKE OPTIONS

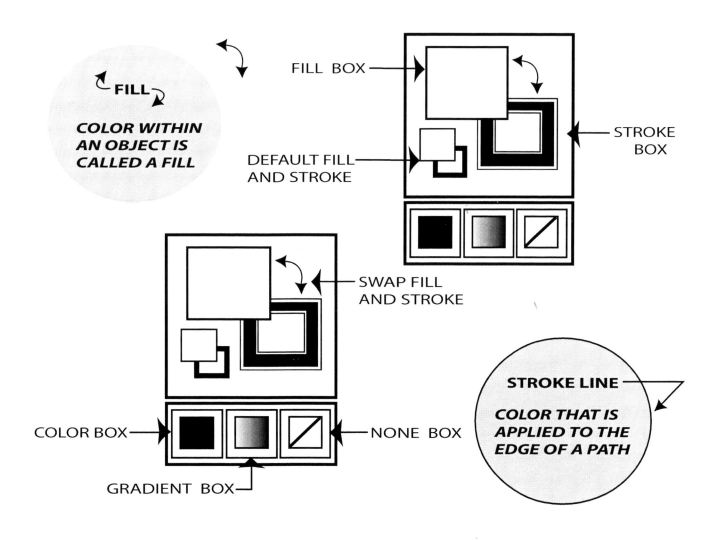

FILL

COLOR WITHIN
AN OBJECT IS
CALLED A FILL

FILL BOX

STROKE
BOX

DEFAULT FILL
AND STROKE

SWAP FILL
AND STROKE

STROKE LINE

COLOR THAT IS
APPLIED TO THE
EDGE OF A PATH

COLOR BOX

NONE BOX

GRADIENT BOX

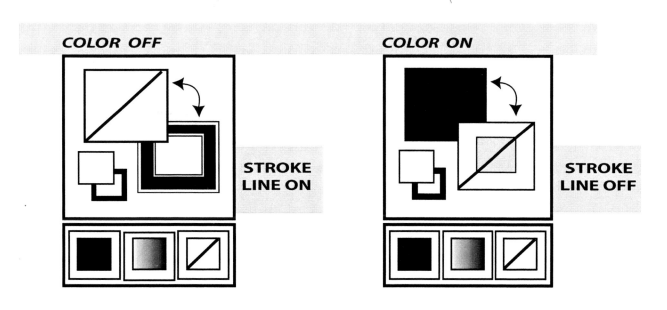

COLOR OFF

COLOR ON

STROKE
LINE ON

STROKE
LINE OFF

STROKE LINES AND DASHED LINES

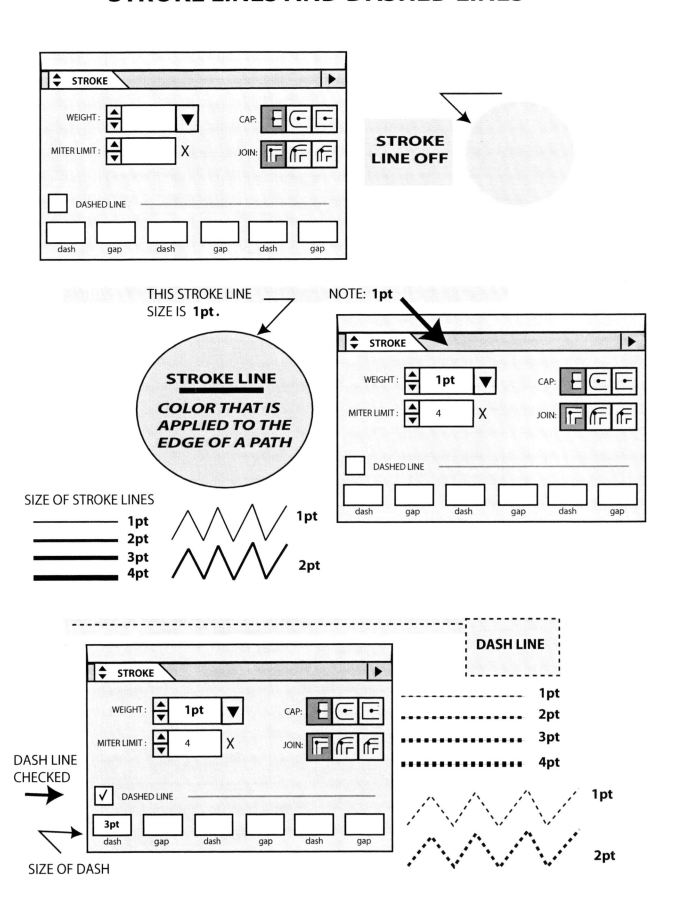

THIS STROKE LINE SIZE IS **1pt.**

NOTE: **1pt**

STROKE LINE OFF

STROKE LINE

COLOR THAT IS APPLIED TO THE EDGE OF A PATH

SIZE OF STROKE LINES

1pt
2pt
3pt
4pt

1pt

2pt

DASH LINE

DASH LINE CHECKED

SIZE OF DASH

DASH LINE

1pt
2pt
3pt
4pt

1pt

2pt

WORKSHEET 1

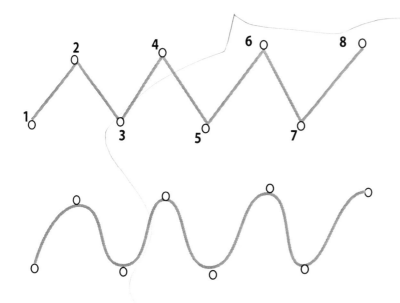

STRAIGHT OPEN PATHS
Lay down 8 anchor points following this image.

.

CURVED OPEN PATHS
Click and drag the points of the straight lines into waves using the Convert Direction Point Tool [↖]. Drag all points to the right. Practice this at least 5 times before moving on to drawing the garments on the following pages.

NOTE:
Anchor points should be pulled in the same direction that they were created.

STRAIGHT LINED CLOSED PATHS
Start by drawing a rectangle with the pen tool. Make sure only the stroke line is on and not the fill. You will need 5 points to make the shape pictured here. Place the 1st point & click to anchor it. Move to the right, click to place anchor point 2. Move down for point 3, go to the left & click for anchor point 4. To close the rectangle with the 5th point, place the cursor over the 1st point and look for the [✎] to close the shape.

CURVED CLOSED PATHS
Go into each open anchor point w/ the Convert Direction Point Tool, [↖] and drag to the right, bending and shaping the straight line into a curved line. When you get to anchor point 3 & 4 drag to the left. If you get a loop line, try to unwind. By practicing this exercise you will gain control of the pen tool and be able to draw the basic garments on the next pages.

GETTING STARTED W/ STRAIGHT LINES

DRAWING STRAIGHT LINES

The simplest kind of line to draw w/ the pen tool is a straight line. Select the pen tool [🖋]. Position the tip of the pen point where you want the straight line to begin, and click to define the first anchor point. The anchor point remains selected [solid ●] until you define the next point. Click again where you want the first segment of the straight line to end [open anchor point ○]. For a single line, deselect the line before continuing or the next point will be attached.

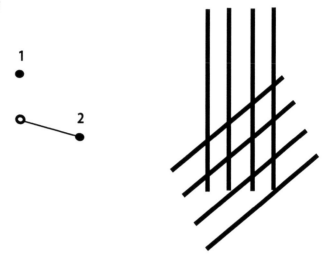

To draw a shape, continue to click and drag additional straight lines to complete these shapes. To close the shape, position the pen pointer over the first anchor point. A small circle will appear next to the pen tip [🖋°] when positioned correctly.

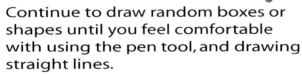 means your on an existing anchor pt.

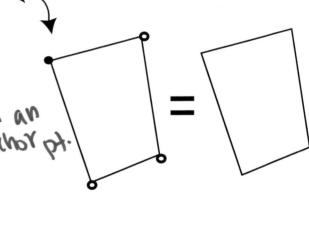

Continue to draw random boxes or shapes until you feel comfortable with using the pen tool, and drawing straight lines.

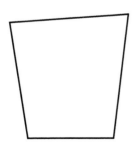

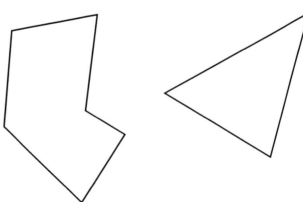

6

SENDING SHAPES TO THE FRONT & BACK

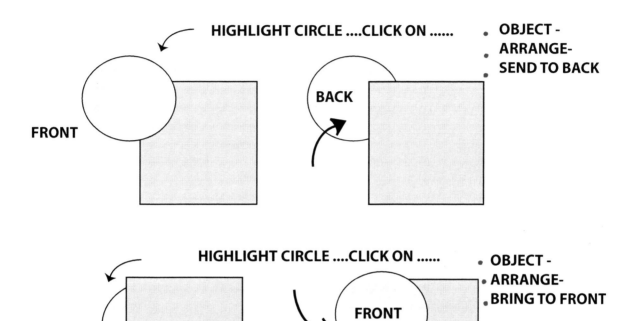

HIGHLIGHT CIRCLE ....CLICK ON ......

FRONT

- OBJECT -
- ARRANGE-
- SEND TO BACK

BACK

HIGHLIGHT CIRCLE ....CLICK ON ......

BACK

FRONT

- OBJECT -
- ARRANGE-
- BRING TO FRONT

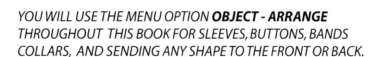

*YOU WILL USE THE MENU OPTION **OBJECT - ARRANGE** THROUGHOUT THIS BOOK FOR SLEEVES, BUTTONS, BANDS COLLARS, AND SENDING ANY SHAPE TO THE FRONT OR BACK.*

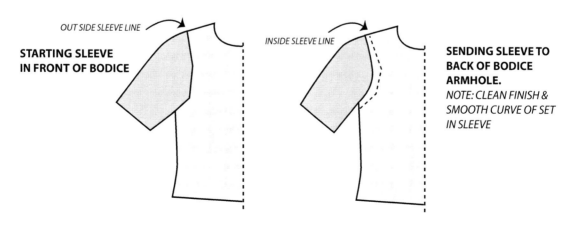

OUT SIDE SLEEVE LINE

STARTING SLEEVE IN FRONT OF BODICE

INSIDE SLEEVE LINE

SENDING SLEEVE TO BACK OF BODICE ARMHOLE.
NOTE: CLEAN FINISH & SMOOTH CURVE OF SET IN SLEEVE

TRANSPARENCY

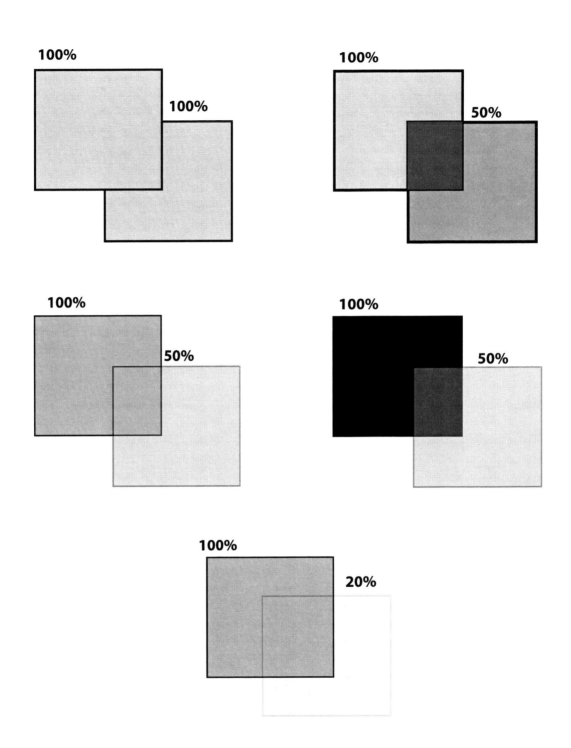

TO USE **TRANSPARENCY** ..... GO TO WINDOW - CLICK ON - **SHOW TRANSPARENCY,** KEEP MENU ON - **NORMAL ..... OPACITY 100% .....** HIGHLIGHT SHAPE ..... **COPY PASTE** A NEW SHAPE, HIGHLIGHT AGAIN AND DRAG THE **OPACITY BAR TO 20% ..... TRY 50%,** SEE WHICH IS BEST FOR THE GARMENT.

TRANSFORMING SHAPES

USING TOOLS AND COMMANDS

OBJECT
TRANSFORM

SCALE

CHANGE THE SIZE OF ANY SHAPE BY USING SCALE

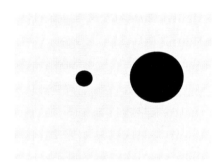

ROTATE

CHANGE THE ANGLE OF A SHAPE BY USING ROTATE

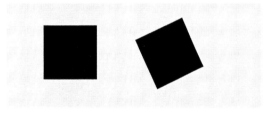

REFLECT

BY USING REFLECT YOU CAN CREATE THE OTHER SIDE OF A SHAPE

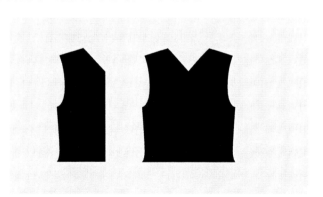

TO USE TRANSFORM
HIGHLIGHT SHAPE FIRST, GO TO
OBJECT- TRANSFORM - SCALE use %
ROTATE use %
REFLECT angle axis

9

WOMEN'S WEAR

WOMEN - BACK CROQUI

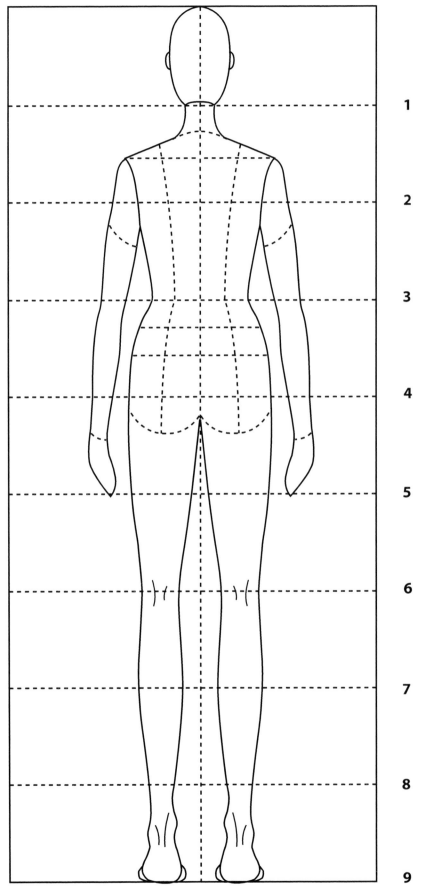

1

2

3

4

5

6

7

8

9

FRONT CROQUI

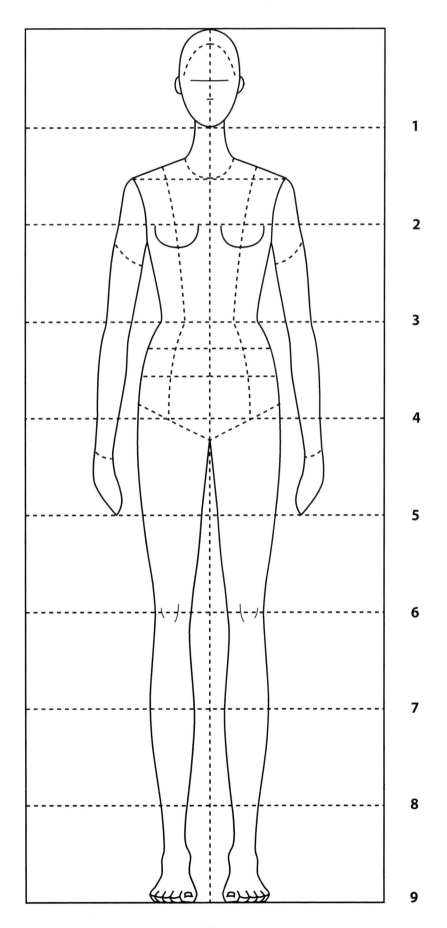

1

2

3

4

5

6

7

8

9

13

WORK SHEET FOR TANK TOP
WOMEN

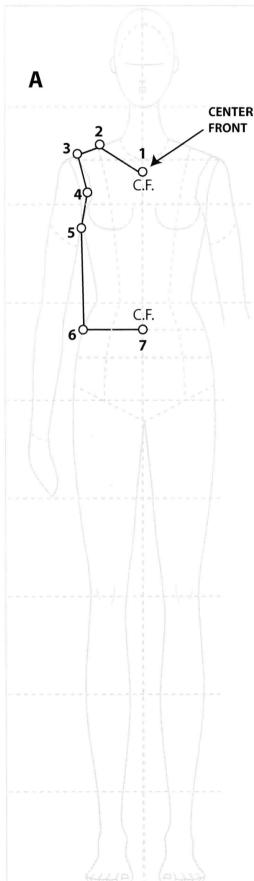

A

CENTER FRONT

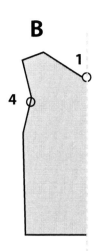

B

C

A   Start w/ your pen tool ....place your **1**st anchor point on C.F. at neckline as pictured to the left. Place anchor point **2** at shoulder, **3** at shoulder/armhole, **4** inside armhole, **5** underarm, **6** at hip side seam and anchor point **7** at hemline, going back to C.F.

B   Using your convert tool [ ] drag open anchor point **1** to the left [to get shape of neckline] drag anchor point **4** down [to get shape of armhole]. Make sure your fill color is on! This makes the process of keeping your C.F. of the garment lined up w/ the dotted line of the croqui. Finish all details on one side before reflecting your top.

Using your direct selection tool [ ], highlight only the open anchor points you want to change. You can do the same process to shape the top, drop the neckline and shorten or lengthen the hemline.

C   This is the shape of the neckline and armhole you would want before reflecting. You can develop the design with added detail after practicing these simple steps several times. This method of clicking and dragging open anchor points to create a shape were used for the garments throughout this book. You may find other ways of developing new styles using this program. I am showing the procedures that work well for Mac's & PC's. After learning the process you can explore short cuts. Eventually you will find your own way.

BASIC TANK TOP

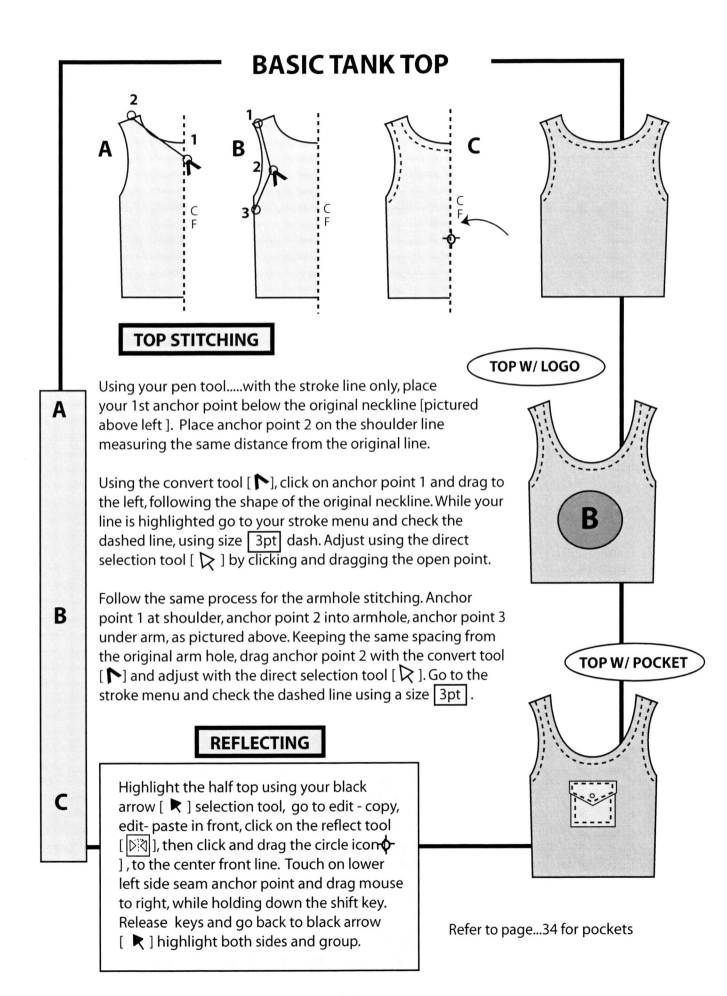

TOP STITCHING

Using your pen tool.....with the stroke line only, place your 1st anchor point below the original neckline [pictured above left]. Place anchor point 2 on the shoulder line measuring the same distance from the original line.

Using the convert tool [ ], click on anchor point 1 and drag to the left, following the shape of the original neckline. While your line is highlighted go to your stroke menu and check the dashed line, using size 3pt dash. Adjust using the direct selection tool [ ] by clicking and dragging the open point.

Follow the same process for the armhole stitching. Anchor point 1 at shoulder, anchor point 2 into armhole, anchor point 3 under arm, as pictured above. Keeping the same spacing from the original arm hole, drag anchor point 2 with the convert tool [ ] and adjust with the direct selection tool [ ]. Go to the stroke menu and check the dashed line using a size 3pt .

REFLECTING

Highlight the half top using your black arrow [ ] selection tool, go to edit - copy, edit- paste in front, click on the reflect tool [ ], then click and drag the circle icon] , to the center front line. Touch on lower left side seam anchor point and drag mouse to right, while holding down the shift key. Release keys and go back to black arrow [ ] highlight both sides and group.

TOP W/ LOGO

TOP W/ POCKET

Refer to page...34 for pockets

15

WORKSHEET FOR SLEEVE
W/ BASIC TOP

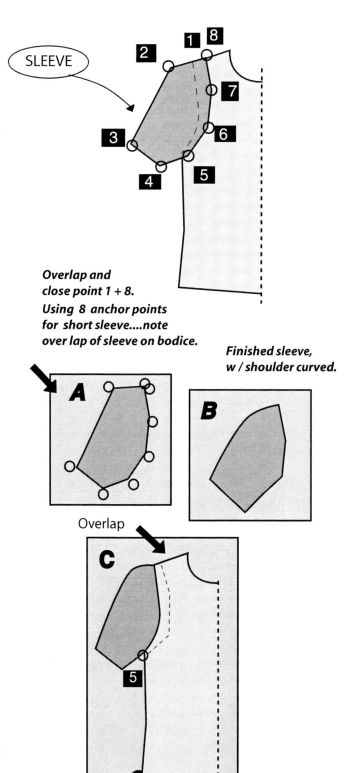

SLEEVE

A After half of the top is done, start your sleeve. Place anchor point 1 on the inside shoulder line, over lapping the armhole (pictured to the right). Move to the left and place anchor point 2 for the shoulder cap, then anchor point 3 for the sleeve hem length. Place anchor point 4 for the inside hemline and anchor point 5 at the side seam of bodice. Anchor points 6 and 7 will overlap the bodice armhole. Anchor point 8 will return to anchor point 1 to close the sleeve.

B Using the convert direction point tool [⌐] click and drag anchor point 2 [shoulder cap] to stretch to the desired curve and shape.

C Click to highlight the sleeve using your black arrow [►] selection tool. Go to object - arrange - send to back. Adjust the lower part of sleeve to fit into armhole by dragging and lifting anchor point 5. Click on the open anchor point with the white arrow [▷] direct selection tool then drag to fit.

You can make many adjustments using your direct selection tool[▷]. Use this tool by clicking on open anchor points and stretching.

REFLECTING

Highlight half of the garment with the black arrow [►] go to edit - copy - edit - paste in front. Highlight the reflect tool [⊠] and move the circle icon [-◇-] on to center front (C.F.). Touch on the lower left side seam anchor point, click and drag to right while holding down shift key to reflect it. Release the keys and go back to black arrow. Highlight both sides and group.

Overlap and close point 1 + 8. Using 8 anchor points for short sleeve....note over lap of sleeve on bodice.

Finished sleeve, w / shoulder curved.

Overlap

Lower left side seam anchor point click and drag to right side, holding down shift key

BASIC T- SHIRT
W / SLEEVE

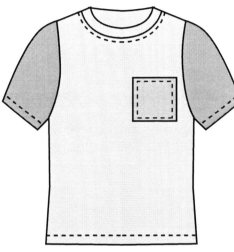

When finished w/ the front view of the garment, you can show the back of the neckline by following these steps.

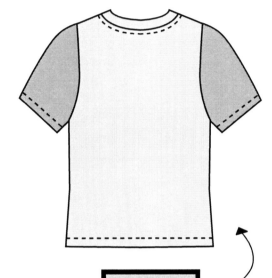

FOR BACK VIEW OF NECKLINE

A Start on C.F. with anchor point 1. Click to the left, past the shoulder/neckline for anchor point 2. Add anchor point 3 on the center line, then back to right shoulder/ neckline for anchor point 4. Close the triangle shape with anchor point 5 by clicking back at the starting point.

B Using the convert tool [↰], drag anchor point 3 to the right and S T R E T C H...to get shape of bottom of neckline piece. To curve the back neckline use the convert tool.

C Click and drag anchor point 1/5 to the right. Use the direct selection tool [▷]dragging down center anchor point.

Highlight w/ selection tool [▶] go to object - arrange - send to back of top, then group the front with the back piece of neckline.

A
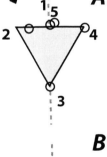

B

C
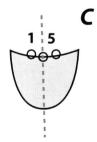

BACK VIEW

To show back view of garment, highlight all parts of front view w/selection tool [▶]. Go to edit copy- edit paste. Using the direct selection tool [▷] highlight and remove any details not necessary for back of garment. Highlight the anchor points you want to change. Conform to back view of croqui to get right effect,by dragging anchor point 1 up on the C.F. line. Continue to do this process for back view of top.

Refer to page...for pockets

WORKSHEET for BLOUSE
W/ COLLAR & CUFFS

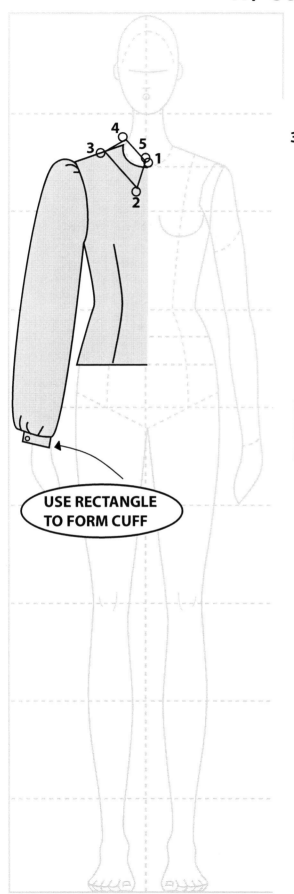

USE RECTANGLE
TO FORM CUFF

After drawing the left side of the blouse place anchor point *1* a bit above the C.F. line, drop down and place anchor point *2*, go up to the shoulder line and place the *3*rd. anchor point, as pictured to the left. *4*th anchor point touching the neck, & closing the collar with anchor point *5*.
To curve collar or reshape, click on anchor point *2*, using the convert tool[↖] and drag to right or left to get desired shape. Now you are ready to reflect.

FOR BACK VIEW OF NECKLINE

A Start on C.F. w/ anchor pt. 1 click & drag anchor pt 2 past the shoulder/neckline, add anchor pt. 3 ,then back to right shoulder/neckline for anchor pt. 4. Finish triangle shape w/anchor pt.5.

B Using convert tool, [↖] drag anchor pt. 3 to right and S T R E T C H ...to get shape of bottom of neckline

C piece. To curve back neckline use the convert [↖] tool into anchor pt. 1 & 5. Drag to right Use direct selection tool [▷] dragging down center anchor point. Highlight w/ selection tool [▶] go to object-arrange - send to back of top, then group the front w/ the back piece of neckline.

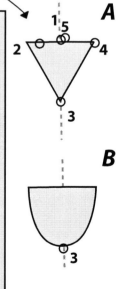

A

B

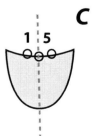

C

BLOUSE W/ COLLAR & CUFFS

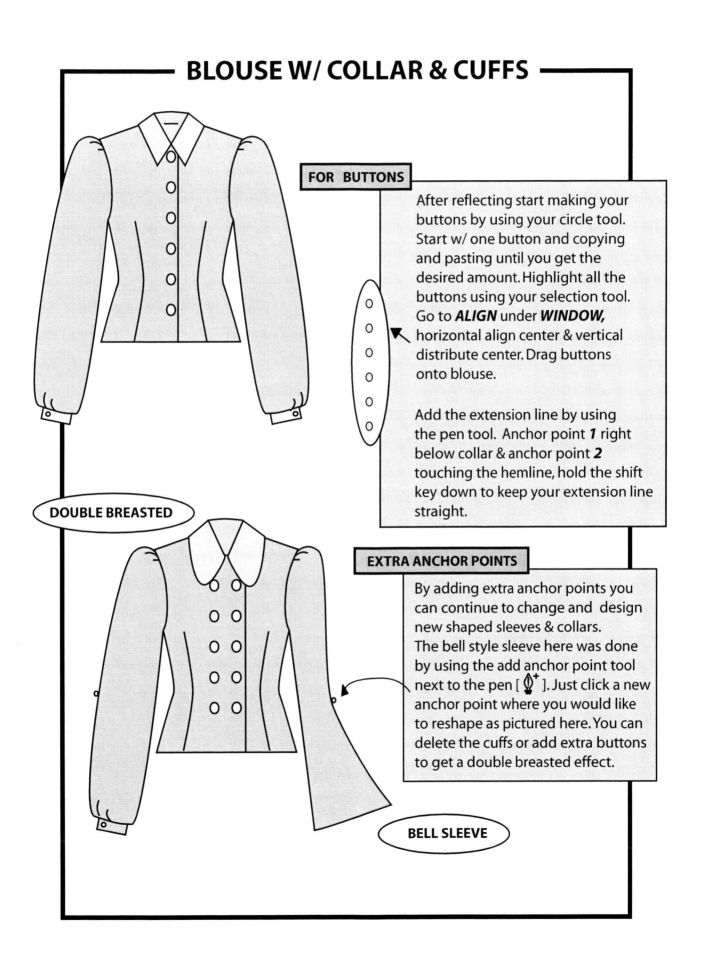

FOR BUTTONS

After reflecting start making your buttons by using your circle tool. Start w/ one button and copying and pasting until you get the desired amount. Highlight all the buttons using your selection tool. Go to **ALIGN** under **WINDOW**, horizontal align center & vertical distribute center. Drag buttons onto blouse.

Add the extension line by using the pen tool. Anchor point **1** right below collar & anchor point **2** touching the hemline, hold the shift key down to keep your extension line straight.

DOUBLE BREASTED

EXTRA ANCHOR POINTS

By adding extra anchor points you can continue to change and design new shaped sleeves & collars. The bell style sleeve here was done by using the add anchor point tool next to the pen [ ]. Just click a new anchor point where you would like to reshape as pictured here. You can delete the cuffs or add extra buttons to get a double breasted effect.

BELL SLEEVE

WORKSHEET FOR PANT

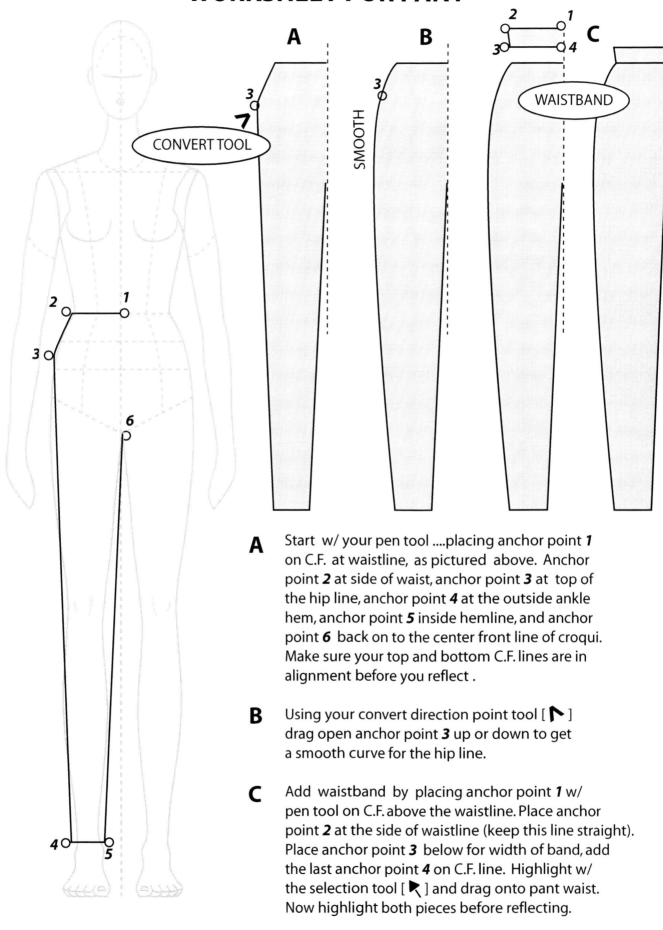

A Start w/ your pen tool ....placing anchor point **1** on C.F. at waistline, as pictured above. Anchor point **2** at side of waist, anchor point **3** at top of the hip line, anchor point **4** at the outside ankle hem, anchor point **5** inside hemline, and anchor point **6** back on to the center front line of croqui. Make sure your top and bottom C.F. lines are in alignment before you reflect .

B Using your convert direction point tool [➤] drag open anchor point **3** up or down to get a smooth curve for the hip line.

C Add waistband by placing anchor point **1** w/ pen tool on C.F. above the waistline. Place anchor point **2** at the side of waistline (keep this line straight). Place anchor point **3** below for width of band, add the last anchor point **4** on C.F. line. Highlight w/ the selection tool [➤] and drag onto pant waist. Now highlight both pieces before reflecting.

BASIC FITTED PANT

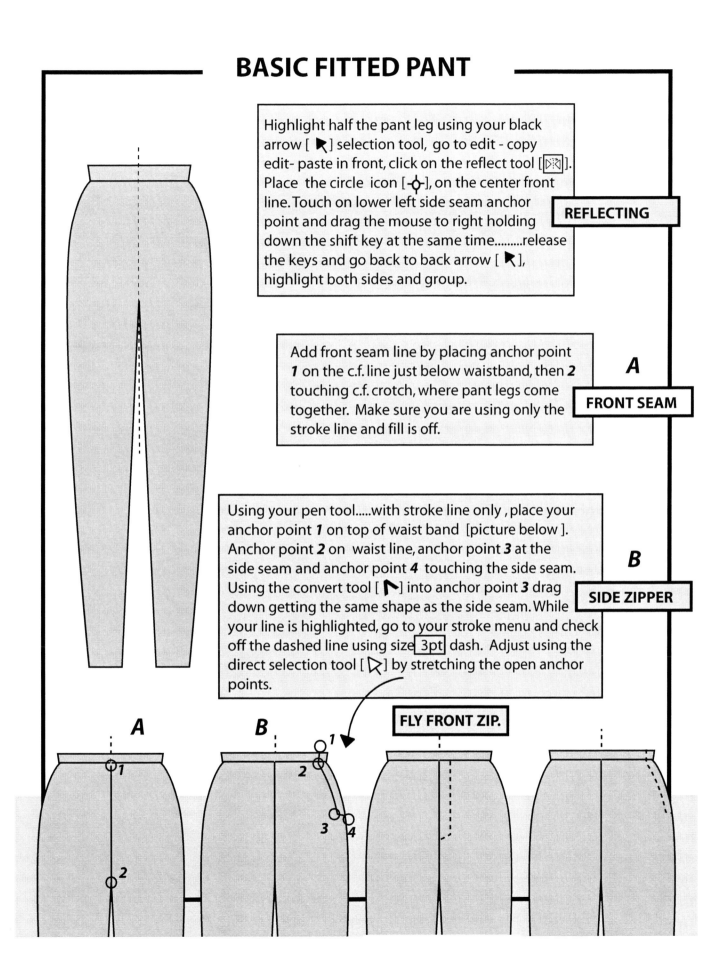

REFLECTING

Highlight half the pant leg using your black arrow [▶] selection tool, go to edit - copy edit- paste in front, click on the reflect tool [▨]. Place the circle icon [-♦-], on the center front line. Touch on lower left side seam anchor point and drag the mouse to right holding down the shift key at the same time.........release the keys and go back to back arrow [▶], highlight both sides and group.

A

FRONT SEAM

Add front seam line by placing anchor point *1* on the c.f. line just below waistband, then *2* touching c.f. crotch, where pant legs come together. Make sure you are using only the stroke line and fill is off.

B

SIDE ZIPPER

Using your pen tool.....with stroke line only , place your anchor point *1* on top of waist band [picture below]. Anchor point *2* on waist line, anchor point *3* at the side seam and anchor point *4* touching the side seam. Using the convert tool [⌐] into anchor point *3* drag down getting the same shape as the side seam. While your line is highlighted, go to your stroke menu and check off the dashed line using size 3pt dash. Adjust using the direct selection tool [▷] by stretching the open anchor points.

A   **B**   **FLY FRONT ZIP.**

1
2
3 *4*

21

WORKSHEET for ELASTIC WAIST SHORT

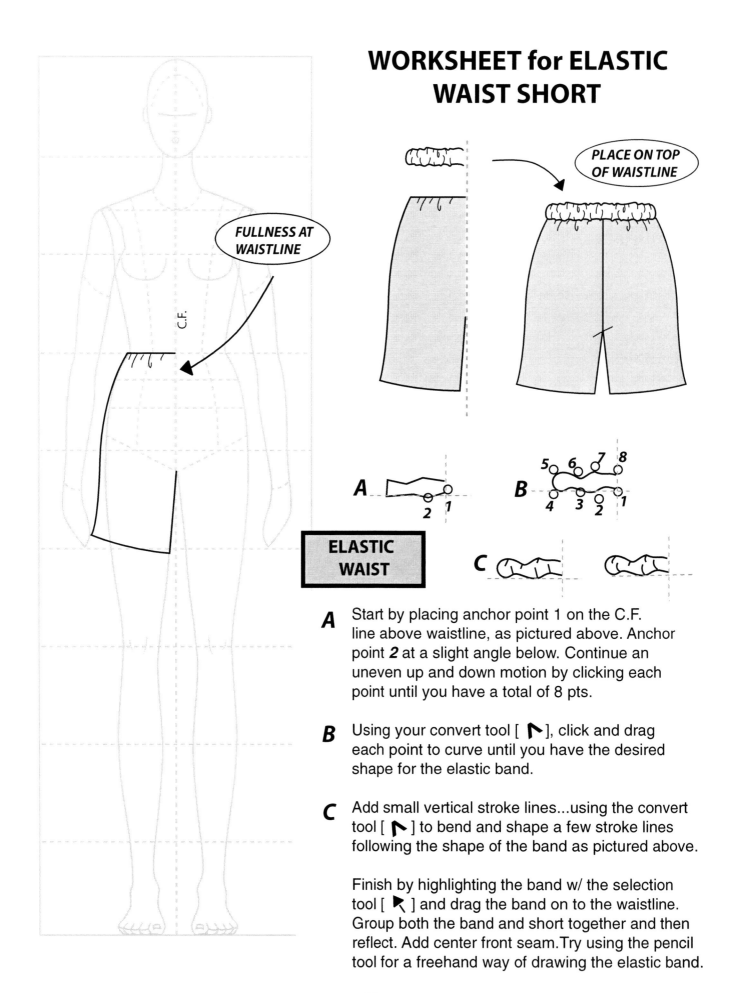

FULLNESS AT WAISTLINE

C.F.

PLACE ON TOP OF WAISTLINE

A

B

5 6 7 8
4 3 2 1

C

ELASTIC WAIST

A Start by placing anchor point 1 on the C.F. line above waistline, as pictured above. Anchor point **2** at a slight angle below. Continue an uneven up and down motion by clicking each point until you have a total of 8 pts.

B Using your convert tool [ ], click and drag each point to curve until you have the desired shape for the elastic band.

C Add small vertical stroke lines...using the convert tool [ ] to bend and shape a few stroke lines following the shape of the band as pictured above.

Finish by highlighting the band w/ the selection tool [ ] and drag the band on to the waistline. Group both the band and short together and then reflect. Add center front seam. Try using the pencil tool for a freehand way of drawing the elastic band.

SHORTS W/ ELASTIC WAIST

DRAWSTRING WAIST

YOKE W/ TOP STITCHING

RACING STRIPE

WORKSHEET FOR FITTED SKIRT

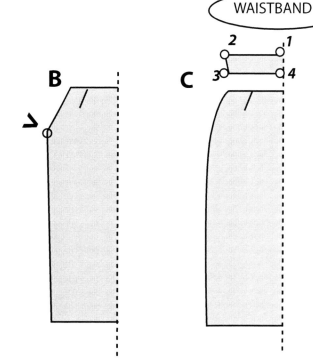

WAISTBAND

B

C

A Start w/ your pen tool ....Place anchor point *1* on the C.F. line at waist, as pictured above. Place anchor point *2* at the side of the waist, anchor point *3* at the top of the hip line, anchor point *4* outside hemline, anchor point *5* back to the center front hemline. Make sure your top and bottom C.F. lines are in alignment before you reflect .

B Using your convert anchor point tool [▶], drag open anchor point *3* up or down to get a smooth curve for the hip line. Using the pen tool add dart for fit.

C Add waistband by placing your anchor point *1* on the C.F. above the waistline, anchor point *2* at the side of the waistline [keep this line straight]. Place anchor point *3* below for the width of the band, add anchor point *4* on the C.F. line. Highlight w/ the selection tool [▶] and drag onto the skirt waist. Select both pieces before reflecting.

BASIC FITTED SKIRT

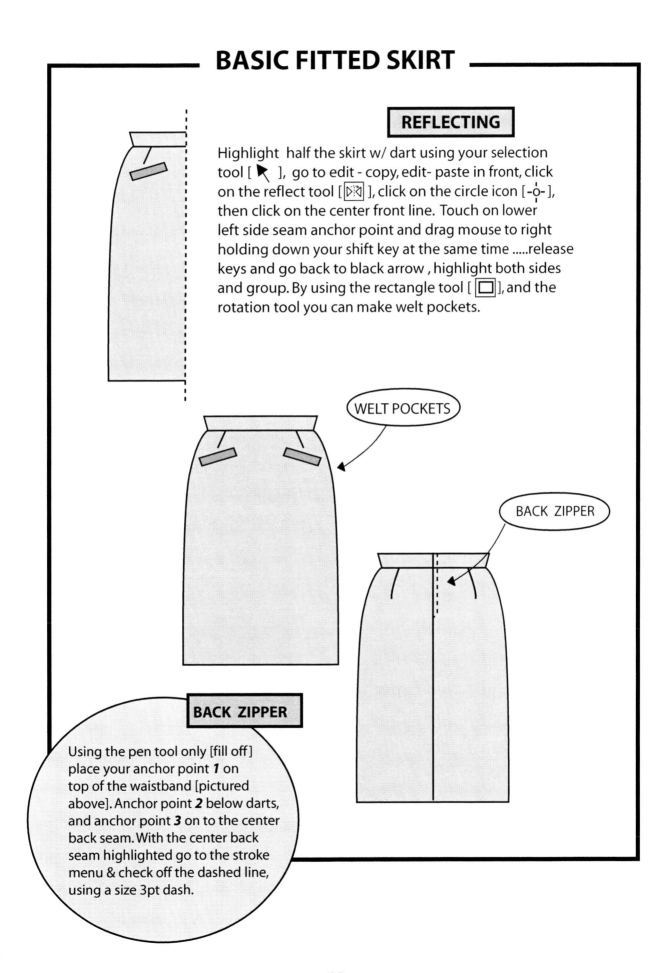

REFLECTING

Highlight half the skirt w/ dart using your selection tool [➤], go to edit - copy, edit- paste in front, click on the reflect tool [⊠], click on the circle icon [-o-], then click on the center front line. Touch on lower left side seam anchor point and drag mouse to right holding down your shift key at the same time .....release keys and go back to black arrow , highlight both sides and group. By using the rectangle tool [☐], and the rotation tool you can make welt pockets.

WELT POCKETS

BACK ZIPPER

BACK ZIPPER

Using the pen tool only [fill off] place your anchor point **1** on top of the waistband [pictured above]. Anchor point **2** below darts, and anchor point **3** on to the center back seam. With the center back seam highlighted go to the stroke menu & check off the dashed line, using a size 3pt dash.

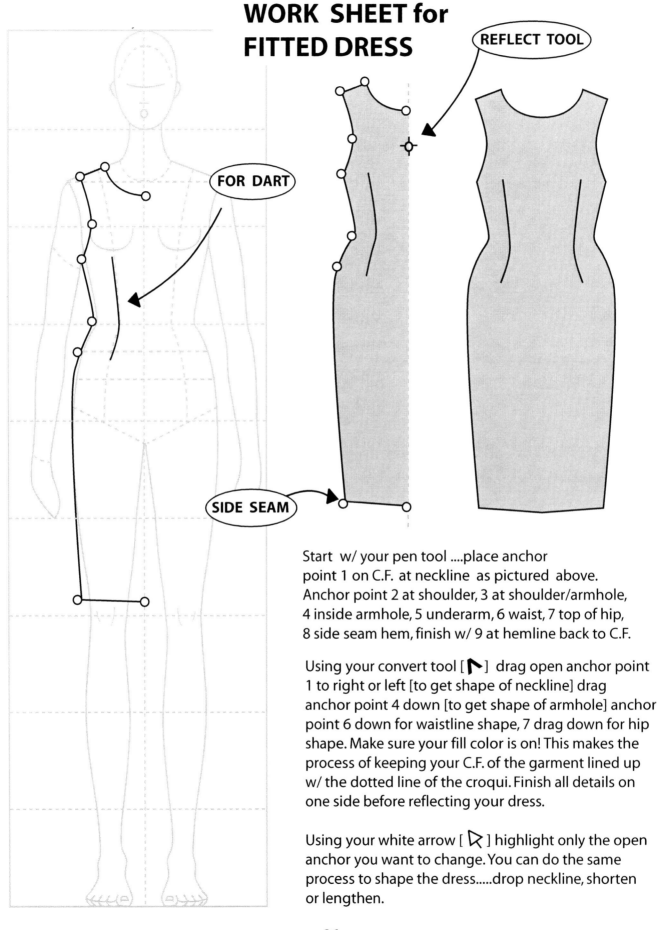

WORK SHEET for FITTED DRESS

REFLECT TOOL

FOR DART

SIDE SEAM

Start w/ your pen tool ....place anchor point 1 on C.F. at neckline as pictured above. Anchor point 2 at shoulder, 3 at shoulder/armhole, 4 inside armhole, 5 underarm, 6 waist, 7 top of hip, 8 side seam hem, finish w/ 9 at hemline back to C.F.

Using your convert tool [ ] drag open anchor point 1 to right or left [to get shape of neckline] drag anchor point 4 down [to get shape of armhole] anchor point 6 down for waistline shape, 7 drag down for hip shape. Make sure your fill color is on! This makes the process of keeping your C.F. of the garment lined up w/ the dotted line of the croqui. Finish all details on one side before reflecting your dress.

Using your white arrow [ ] highlight only the open anchor you want to change. You can do the same process to shape the dress.....drop neckline, shorten or lengthen.

BASIC FITTED DRESS

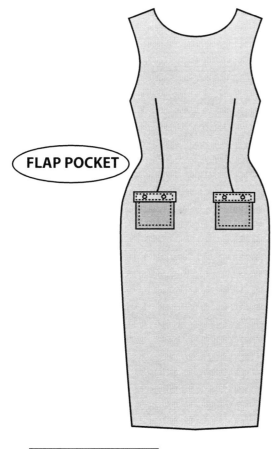

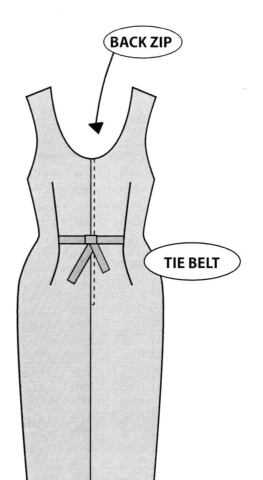

FLAP POCKET

BACK ZIP

TIE BELT

REFLECTING

Highlight half the dress w/ dart using your black
arrow [selection tool], go to edit - copy
edit- paste in front, click on the reflect tool [⋈]
click on the circle icon [⟡], then click on
the center front line. Touch on lower
left side seam anchor point and drag
mouse to right holding down your shift
key at the same time .... release keys
and go back to black arrow, highlight
both sides and group.

Refer to page34
for pockets

BACK ZIPPER

Using your pen tool......place your anchor point 1
at the top of the back neckline just to the right of the C.B. seam.
Place anchor point 2 where the bottom of the zipper will be. Place
anchor point 3 on the back seam. Go to your stroke menu and check
off the dashed box, use size 3 dashed line for back zipper.

RUFFLES

Start by using the rectangle shape as a guide.

Start with anchor point *1* a little in on the top line. Place anchor point *2* on the bottom line for ruffle hemline, anchor point *3* on the same line. Move to the middle of the rectangle and place anchor point *4.* Moving slightly above and to the right place anchor point *5.* Repeat the process starting below the last point.

Drag the open anchor points using the convert direction point tool [➤] to the right to curve the lines and create an image of fullness.

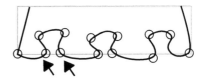

On the top of each curve add a line by using your pen tool. Finish by adding short lines inbetween the folds.

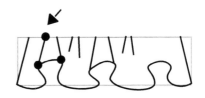

Keep the folds uneven.

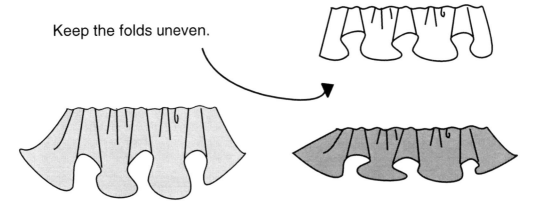

RUFFLE SEPARATES

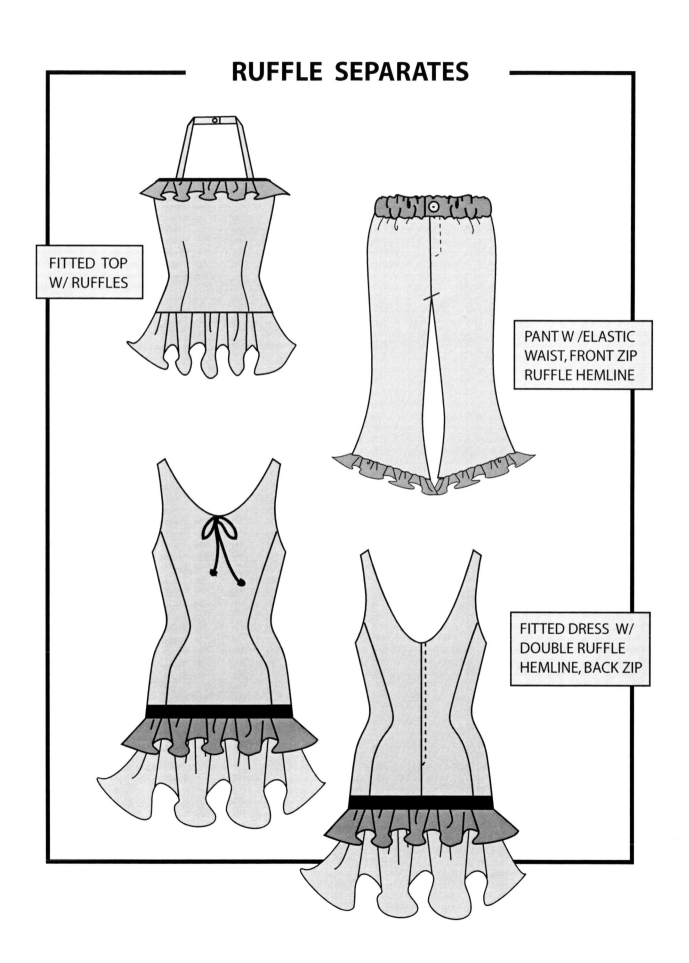

FITTED TOP
W/ RUFFLES

PANT W /ELASTIC
WAIST, FRONT ZIP
RUFFLE HEMLINE

FITTED DRESS W/
DOUBLE RUFFLE
HEMLINE, BACK ZIP

WORK SHEET FOR RUFFLE TOP

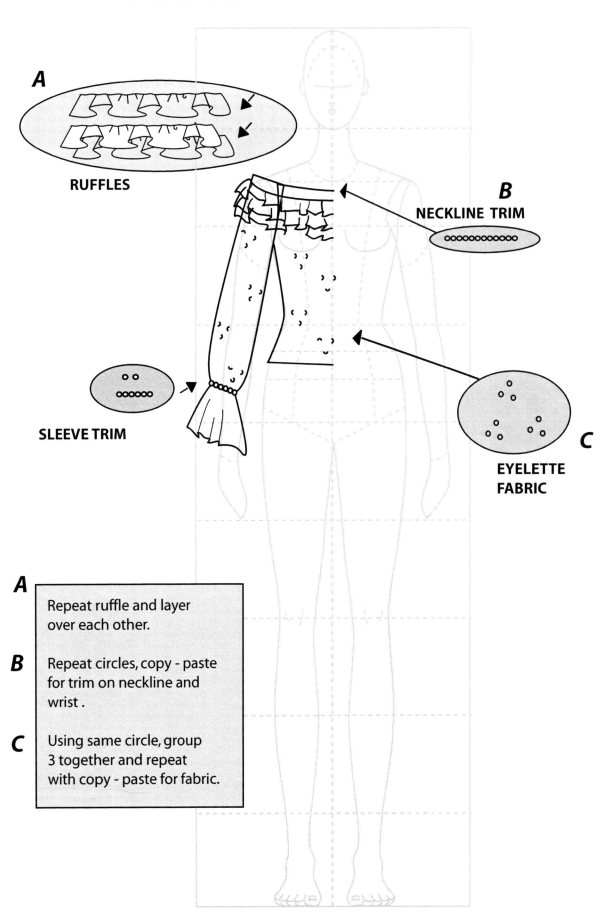

A

RUFFLES

B

NECKLINE TRIM

SLEEVE TRIM

C

EYELETTE
FABRIC

A Repeat ruffle and layer over each other.

B Repeat circles, copy - paste for trim on neckline and wrist .

C Using same circle, group 3 together and repeat with copy - paste for fabric.

TOP W/ RUFFLE NECKLINE

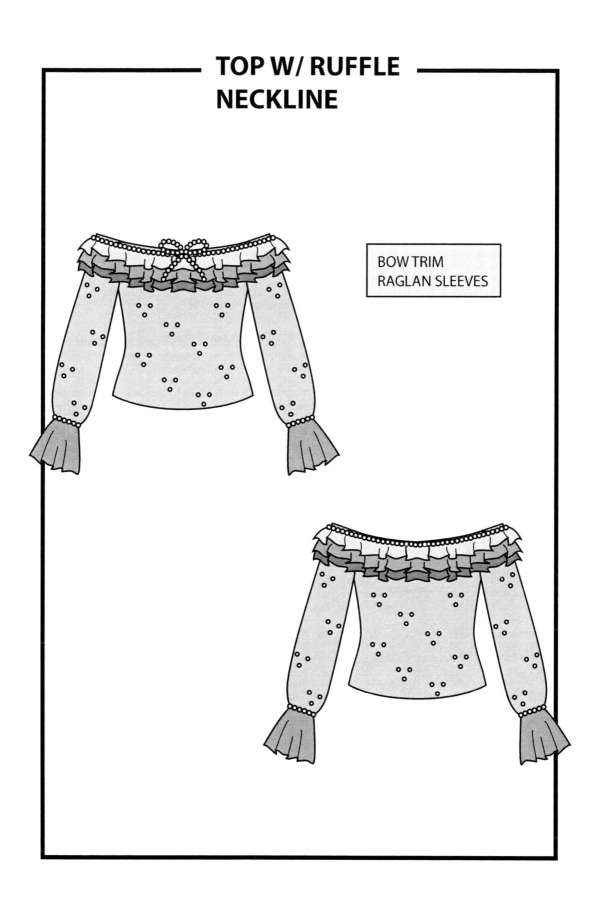

BOW TRIM
RAGLAN SLEEVES

HOOD WORKSHEET

START BY PLACING 6 ANCHOR POINTS.
AS SHOWN...ANCHOR POINT 1 AND
ANCHOR POINT 6 START AND END ON
THE CENTER FRONT.

CURVE ANCHOR POINTS 1 ..2..3..& 4.
ADJUST SHAPE W/ WHITE ARROW
(DIRECT SELECTION TOOL)

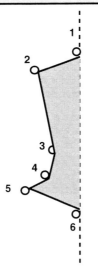

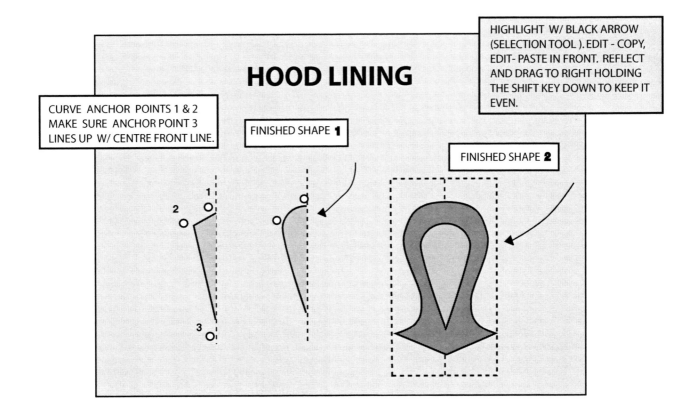

HOOD LINING

HIGHLIGHT W/ BLACK ARROW
(SELECTION TOOL). EDIT - COPY,
EDIT- PASTE IN FRONT. REFLECT
AND DRAG TO RIGHT HOLDING
THE SHIFT KEY DOWN TO KEEP IT
EVEN.

CURVE ANCHOR POINTS 1 & 2
MAKE SURE ANCHOR POINT 3
LINES UP W/ CENTRE FRONT LINE.

FINISHED SHAPE **1**

FINISHED SHAPE **2**

HOODS

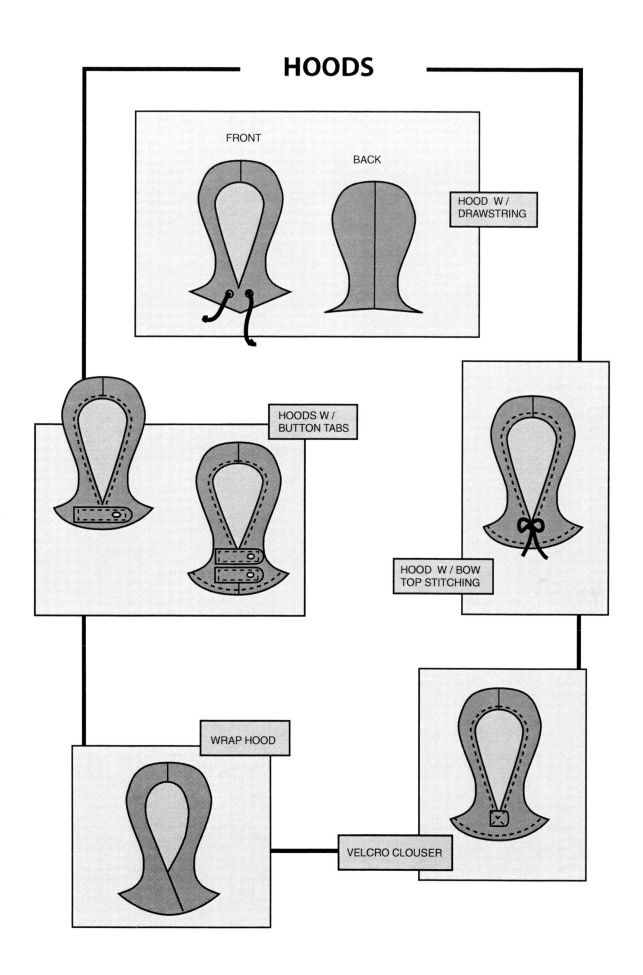

FRONT

BACK

HOOD W / DRAWSTRING

HOODS W / BUTTON TABS

HOOD W / BOW TOP STITCHING

WRAP HOOD

VELCRO CLOUSER

PATCH POCKET WORKSHEET

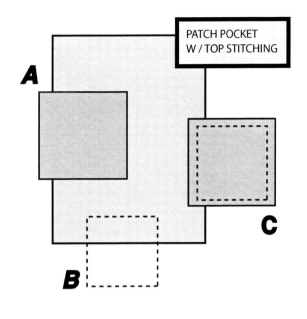

A

PATCH POCKET
W / TOP STITCHING

C

B

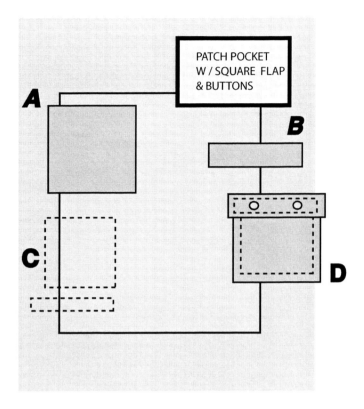

A

PATCH POCKET
W / SQUARE FLAP
& BUTTONS

B

C

D

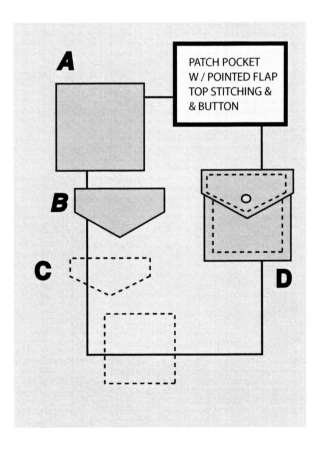

A

PATCH POCKET
W / POINTED FLAP
TOP STITCHING &
& BUTTON

B

C

D

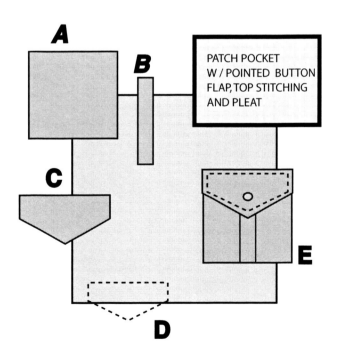

A

B

PATCH POCKET
W / POINTED BUTTON
FLAP, TOP STITCHING
AND PLEAT

C

D

E

INDUSTRIAL ZIPPER WORKSHEET

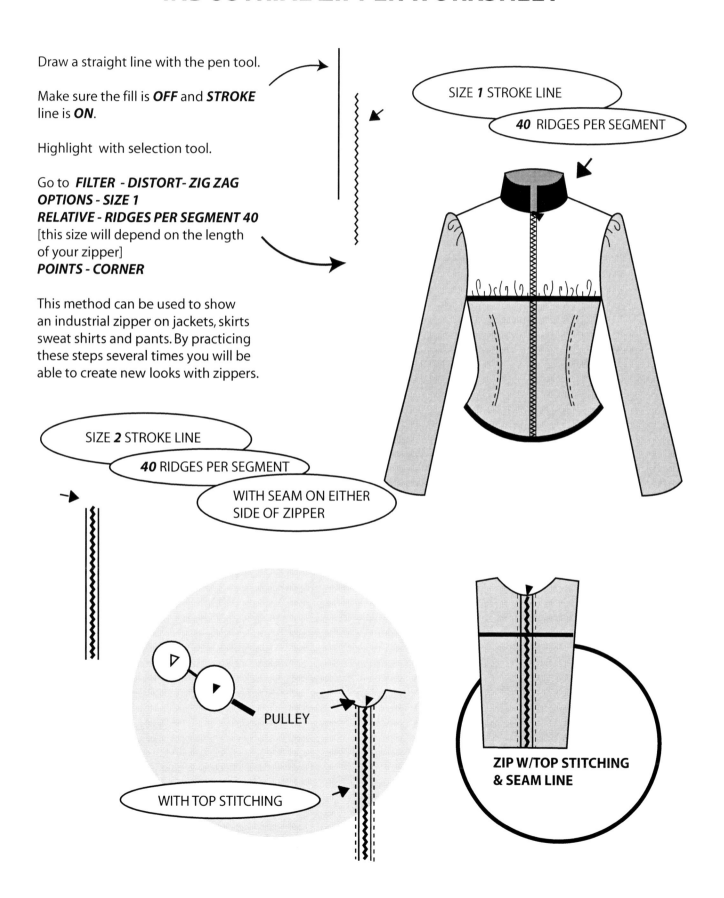

Draw a straight line with the pen tool.

Make sure the fill is **OFF** and **STROKE** line is **ON**.

Highlight with selection tool.

Go to **FILTER - DISTORT - ZIG ZAG**
OPTIONS - SIZE 1
RELATIVE - RIDGES PER SEGMENT 40
[this size will depend on the length of your zipper]
POINTS - CORNER

This method can be used to show an industrial zipper on jackets, skirts sweat shirts and pants. By practicing these steps several times you will be able to create new looks with zippers.

SIZE **1** STROKE LINE

40 RIDGES PER SEGMENT

SIZE **2** STROKE LINE

40 RIDGES PER SEGMENT

WITH SEAM ON EITHER SIDE OF ZIPPER

PULLEY

WITH TOP STITCHING

ZIP W/TOP STITCHING & SEAM LINE

TANK TOP / STRIPES

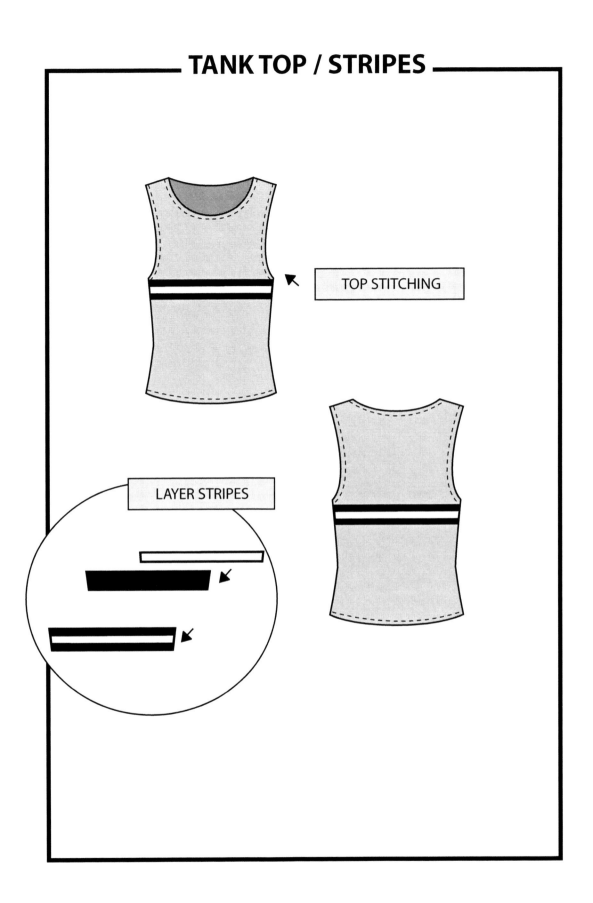

TOP STITCHING

LAYER STRIPES

CAMISOLE TOP
W/ LACE TRIM

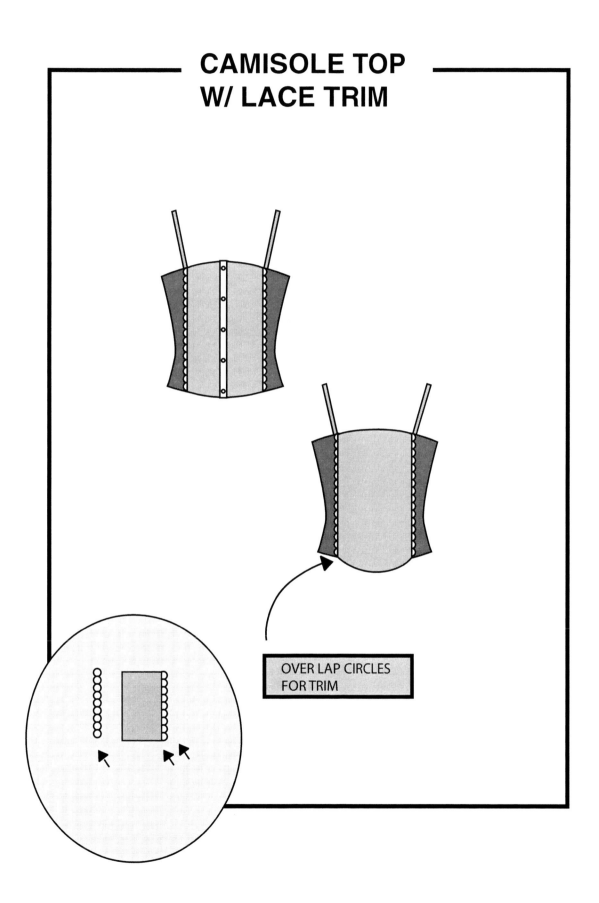

OVER LAP CIRCLES
FOR TRIM

PEASANT TOP W/ RAGLAN SLEEVES

FOR PRINT USE
CIRCLES AND
REPEAT

TOP W/ V NECKLINE & LAYERED COLLAR

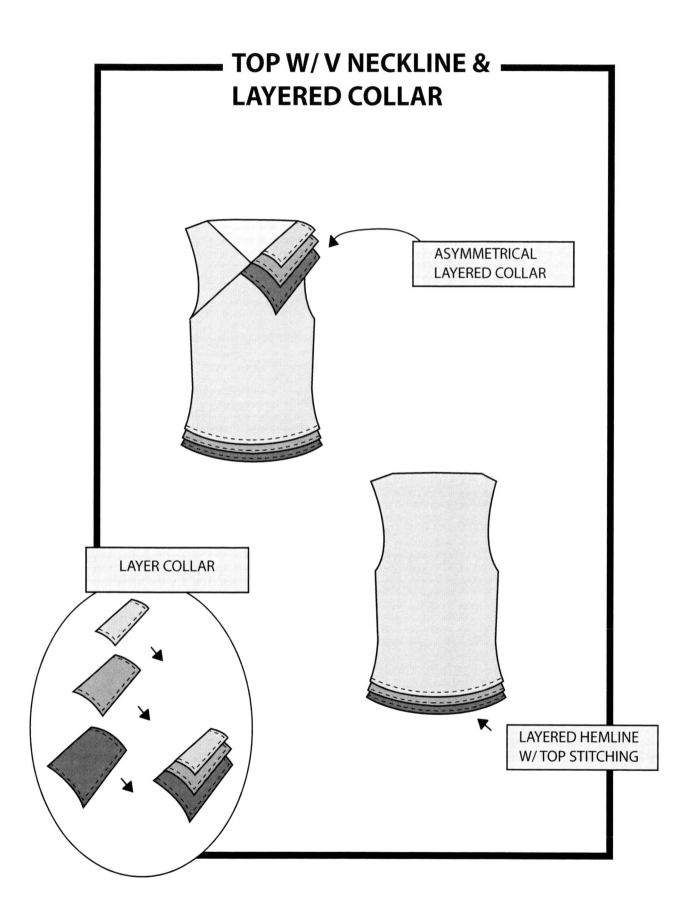

ASYMMETRICAL LAYERED COLLAR

LAYER COLLAR

LAYERED HEMLINE W/ TOP STITCHING

TOP W/ DECORATIVE TRIM & BOW

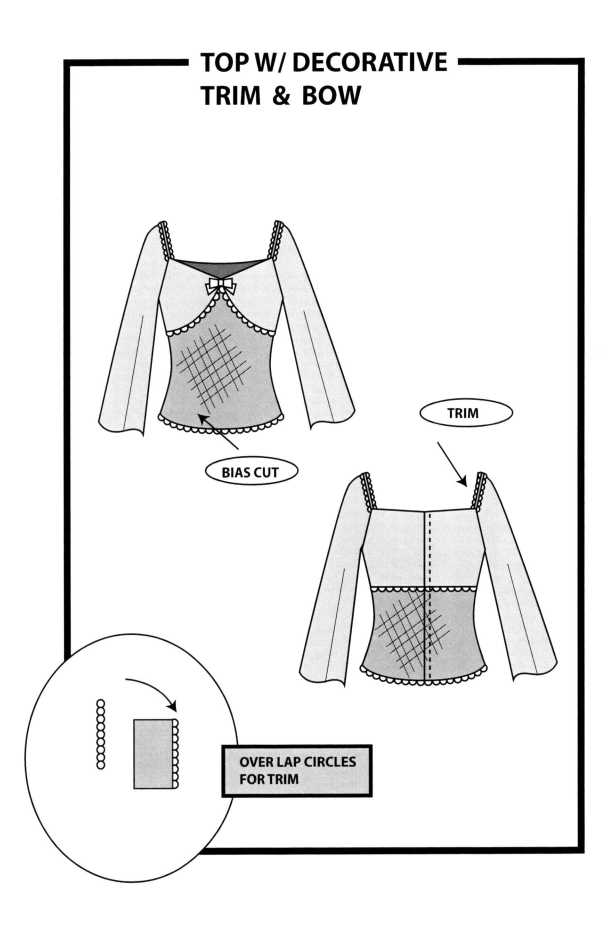

TRIM

BIAS CUT

OVER LAP CIRCLES
FOR TRIM

GATHERED TOP W/ RUFFLED STRAPS

GATHERED BODICE

TOP W/ BUTTON
FRONT & TRIM

TRIM

FOR
TRIM

**USE ZIG ZAG TOOL
UNDER EFFECT /
DISTORT**

FITTED BLOUSE W/ CORSET STYLING

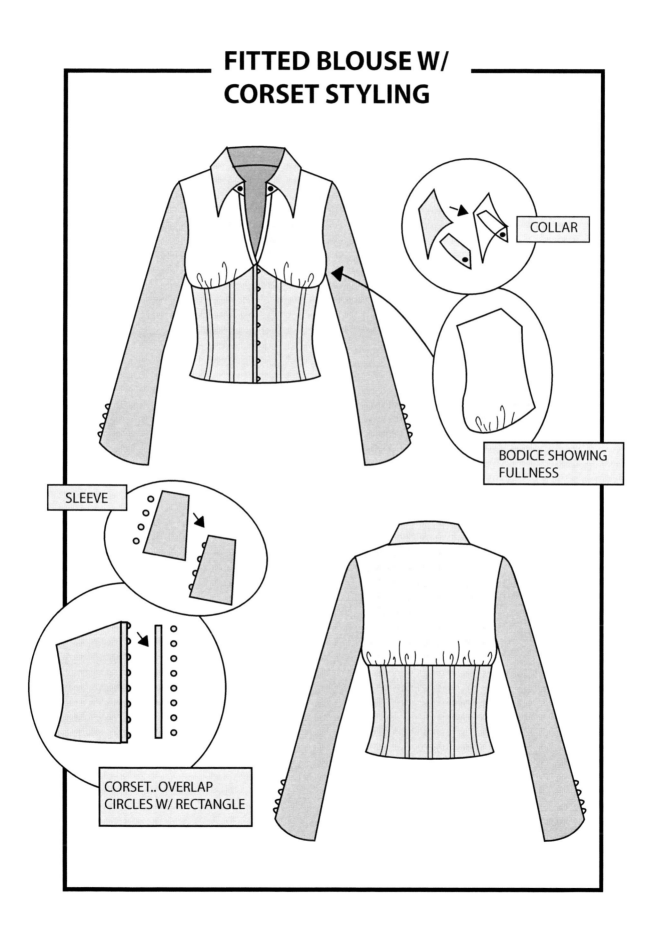

COLLAR

BODICE SHOWING FULLNESS

SLEEVE

CORSET.. OVERLAP CIRCLES W/ RECTANGLE

43

PANT W/ POCKETS AND SIDE SLITS

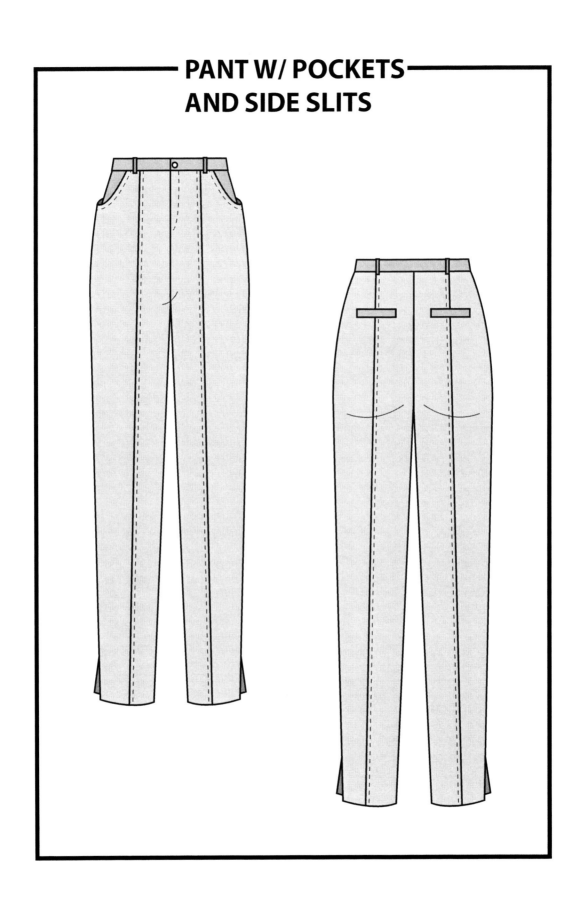

FIT & FLARE JEAN
STYLE PANT

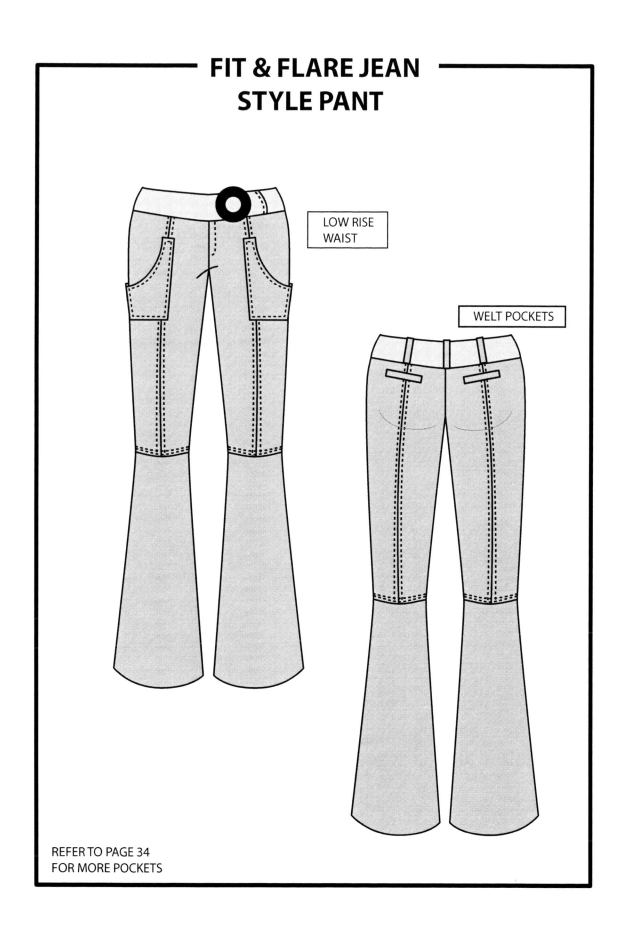

LOW RISE WAIST

WELT POCKETS

REFER TO PAGE 34
FOR MORE POCKETS

JEAN STYLE PANT

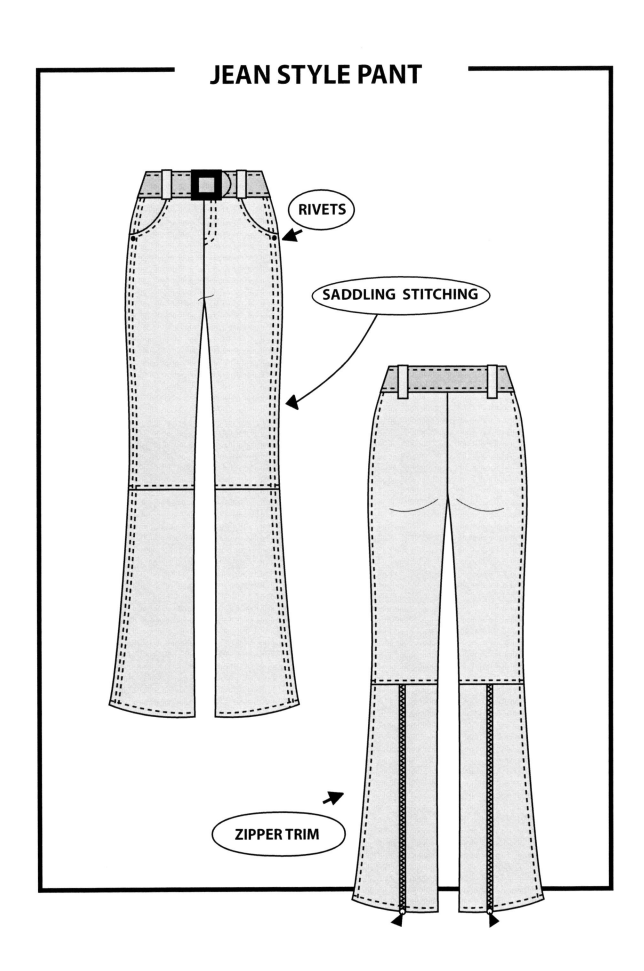

RIVETS

SADDLING STITCHING

ZIPPER TRIM

ELASTIC WAIST PANT
W/ DRAWSTRING

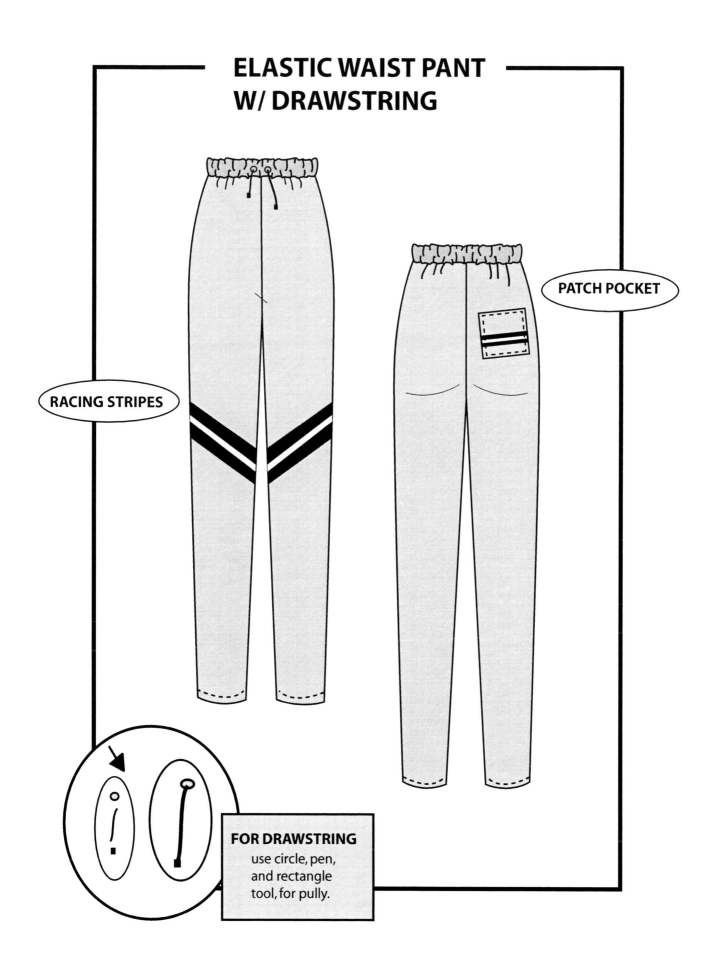

RACING STRIPES

PATCH POCKET

FOR DRAWSTRING
use circle, pen, and rectangle tool, for pully.

SHORTS W/ ELASTIC WAIST AND RUFFLES

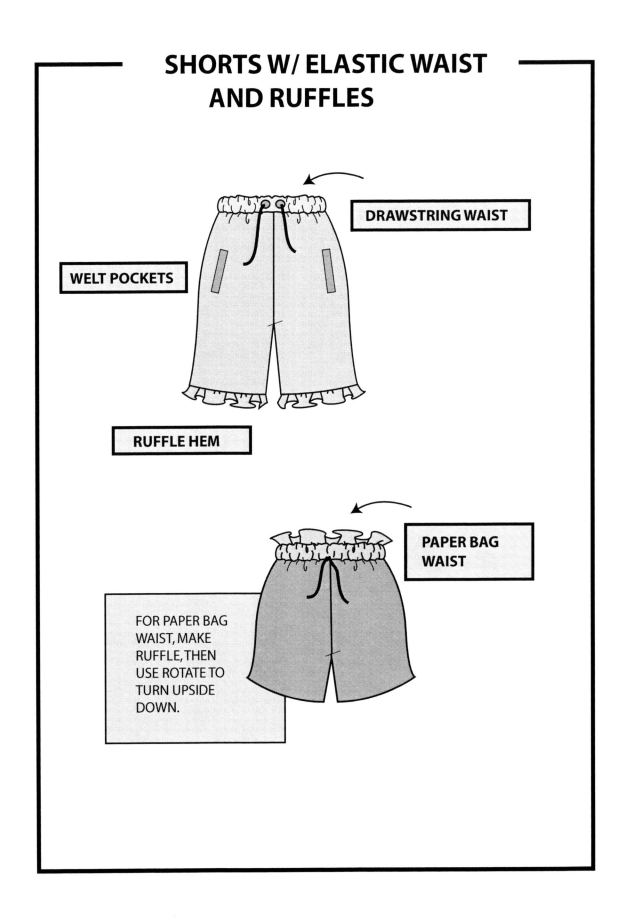

DRAWSTRING WAIST

WELT POCKETS

RUFFLE HEM

PAPER BAG WAIST

FOR PAPER BAG WAIST, MAKE RUFFLE, THEN USE ROTATE TO TURN UPSIDE DOWN.

SHORTS W/ ELASTIC WAIST

YOKE W/SADDLE
STITCHING

FLARE STYLE SHORTS
W/ PATCH POCKETS

WELT POCKETS
FLY FRONT ZIP
AND CUFFS

A-LINE SKIRT W/ INVERTED PLEAT

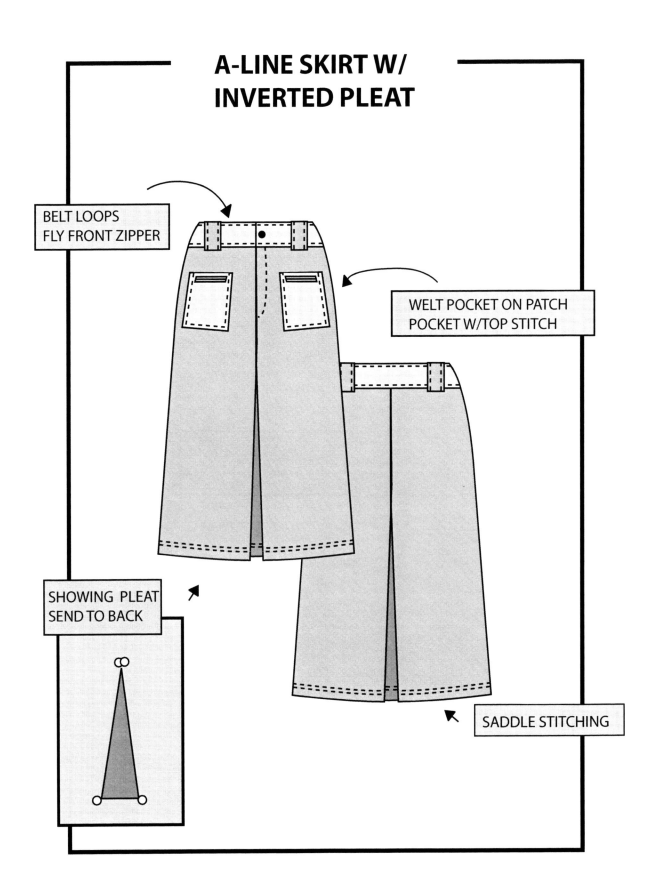

BELT LOOPS
FLY FRONT ZIPPER

WELT POCKET ON PATCH
POCKET W/TOP STITCH

SHOWING PLEAT
SEND TO BACK

SADDLE STITCHING

KNIFE PLEATED SKIRT
W/ WIDE WAISTBAND

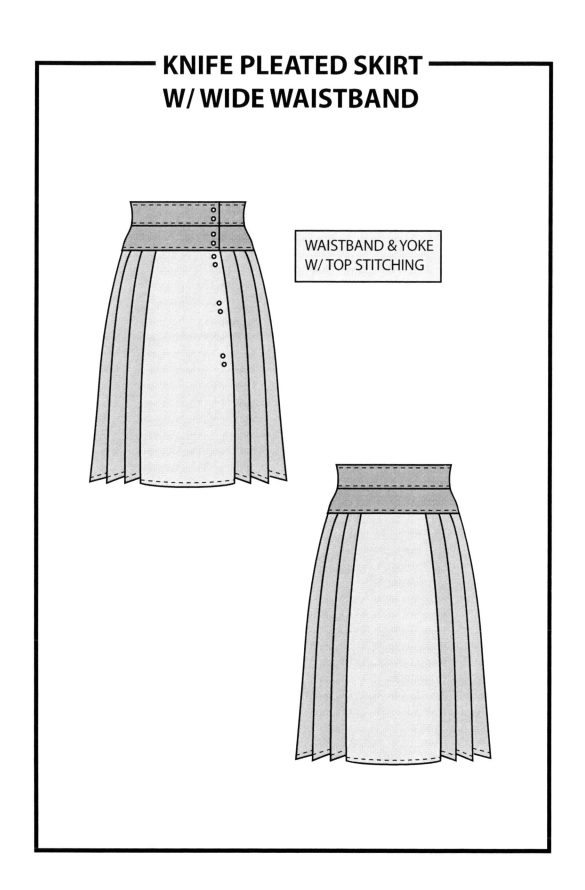

WAISTBAND & YOKE
W/ TOP STITCHING

FIT & FLARE SKIRT W/ FRONT POCKETS

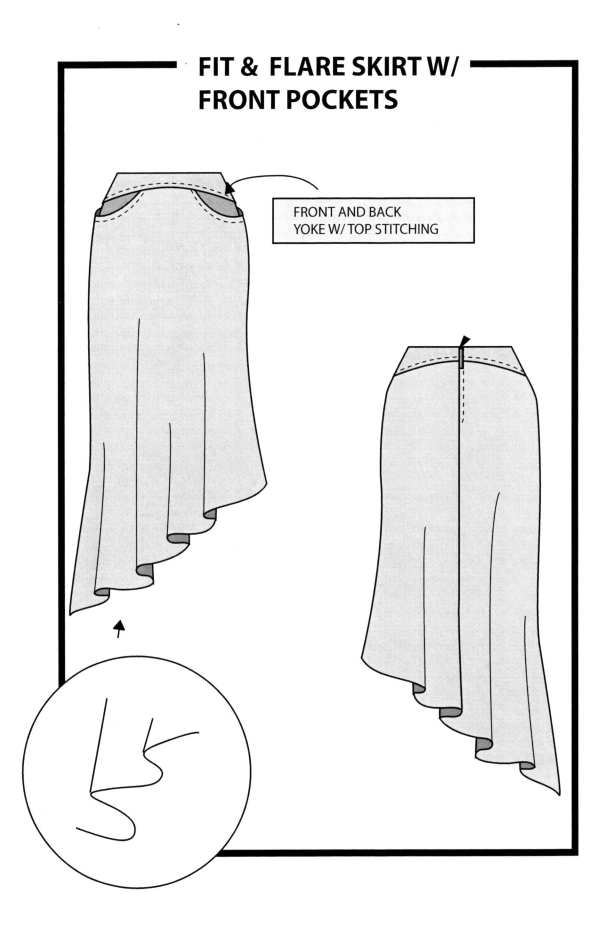

FRONT AND BACK
YOKE W/ TOP STITCHING

FIT & FLARE SKIRT

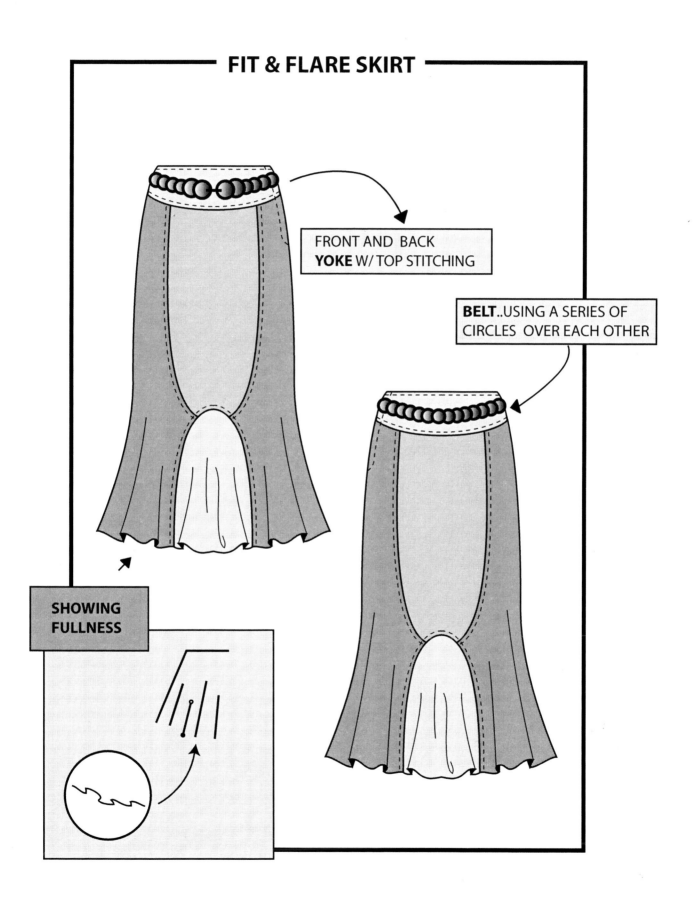

FRONT AND BACK
YOKE W/ TOP STITCHING

BELT..USING A SERIES OF
CIRCLES OVER EACH OTHER

**SHOWING
FULLNESS**

CORSET STYLE DRESS

HOOK & EYE
FRONT CLOSING

SLEEVELESS DRESS
W/ COLLAR

BUTTON OPENING
W/ EMPIRE WAIST

SADDLE STITCH
HEMLINE

FITTED JACKET W/
STAND UP COLLAR

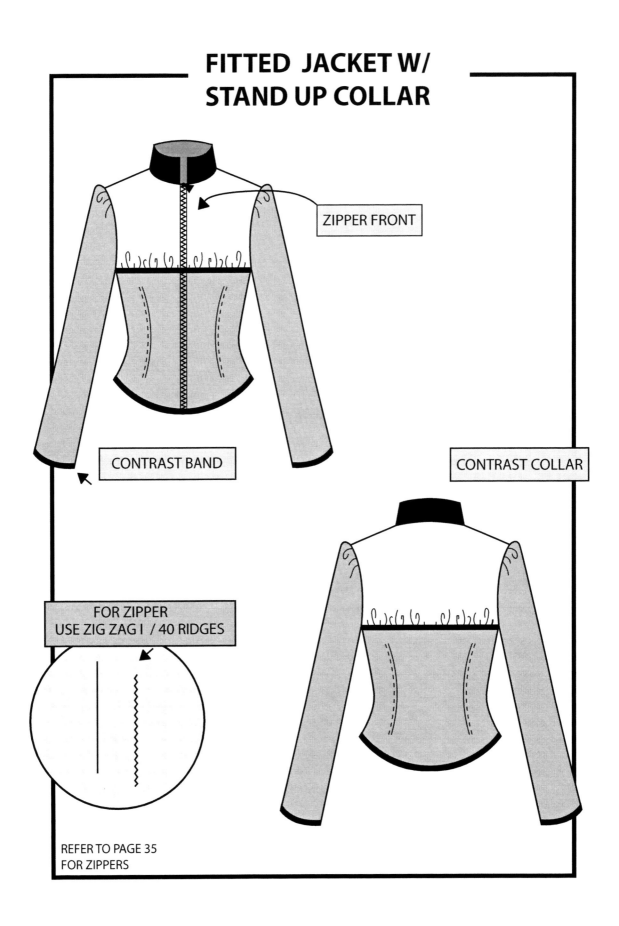

ZIPPER FRONT

CONTRAST BAND

CONTRAST COLLAR

FOR ZIPPER
USE ZIG ZAG I / 40 RIDGES

REFER TO PAGE 35
FOR ZIPPERS

FITTED JACKET W/ NOTCHED COLLAR

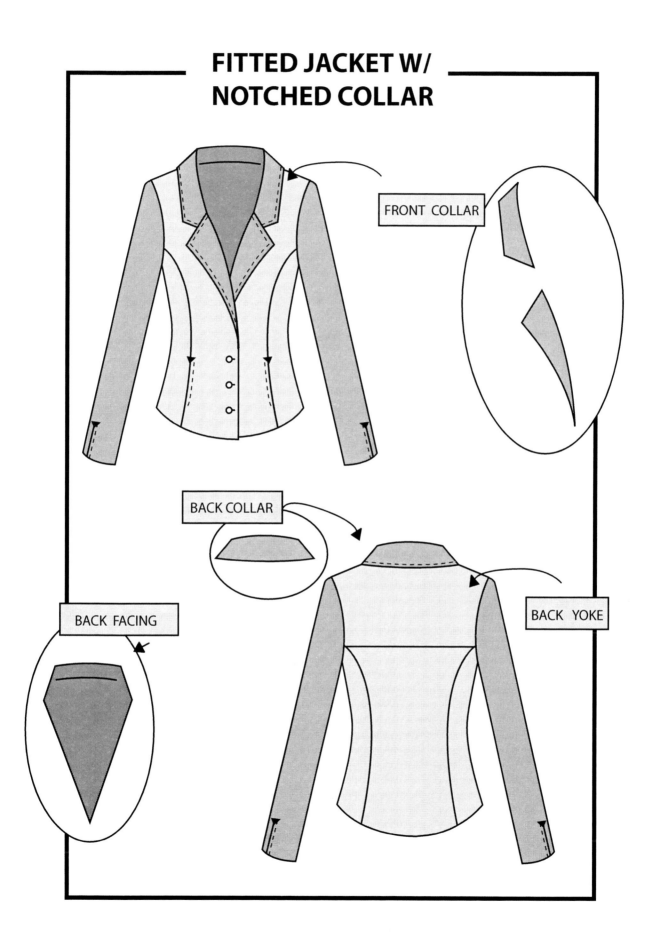

FRONT COLLAR

BACK COLLAR

BACK FACING

BACK YOKE

JACKET W/ HOOD & COLOR BLOCKING

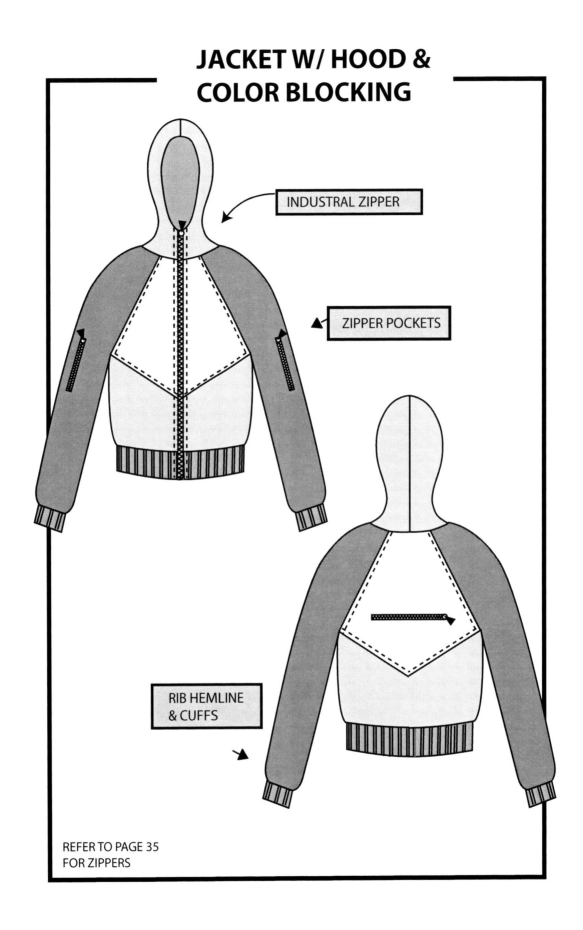

INDUSTRAL ZIPPER

ZIPPER POCKETS

RIB HEMLINE & CUFFS

REFER TO PAGE 35
FOR ZIPPERS

BIKER JACKET

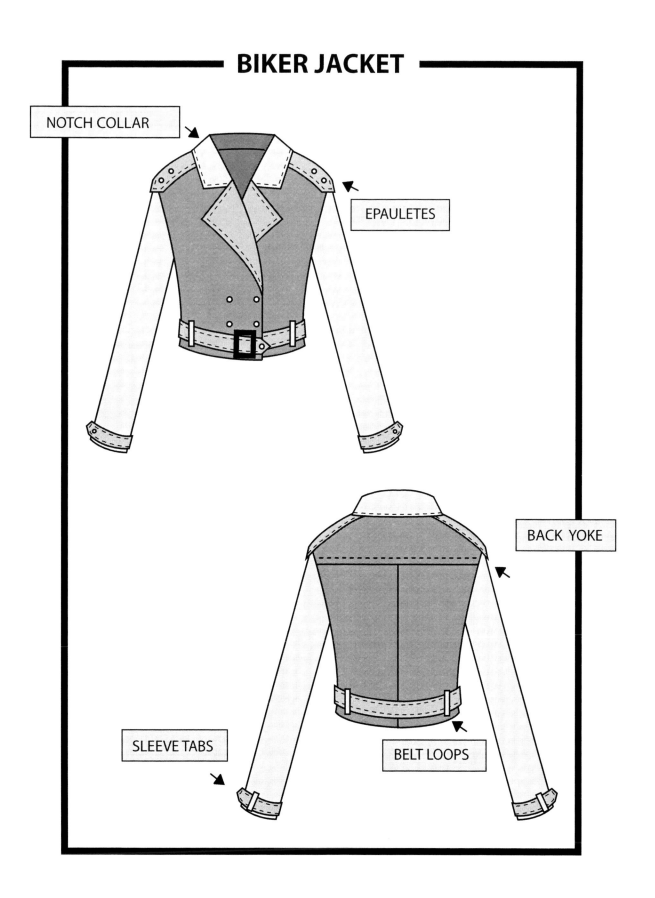

NOTCH COLLAR

EPAULETES

BACK YOKE

SLEEVE TABS

BELT LOOPS

INFANTS
KIDS WEAR

INFANT

FRONT / BACK CROQUIS

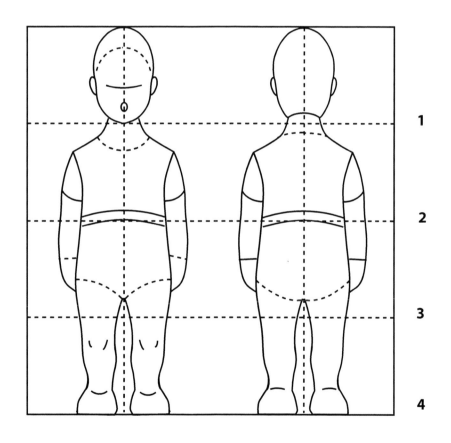

1

2

3

4

WORK SHEET FOR INFANTS TANK TOP

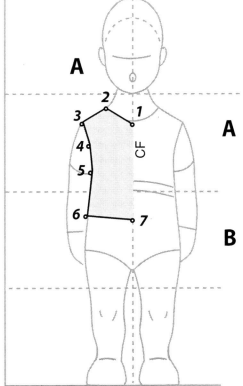

A

CF

2
3
1
4
5
6
7

TOP

A Start w/ your pen tool ..... place anchor point *1* on C.F. at neckline as pictured above. Anchor point *2* at shoulder, anchor point *3* at shoulder/armhole, anchor point *4* inside armhole, anchor point *5* underarm, anchor point *6* at the hip side seam, and anchor point *7* at hemline on C.F.

B Using your convert tool [✎] drag open anchor point *1* to the right or left to get the shape of the neckline. Drag anchor point *4* down to get shape of the armhole. Make sure your fill color is on! This makes the process of keeping your C.F. of the garment lined up w/ the dotted line of the croqui. Finish all details on one side before reflecting your top.

Using your white arrow, direct selection tool [➤], highlight only the open anchor point that you want to adjust. You can do the same process to shape the top.....drop neckline and shorten or lengthen hemline.

This is the shape of the neckline and the armhole you would want before reflecting. You can develop the design with added detail, after practicing these simple steps several times. This method of clicking and dragging open anchor points to create a shape was used for the styles throughout this book. There are many ways of developing new styles using this program, I am showing what I think is the simplest way. Eventually you will find your own.

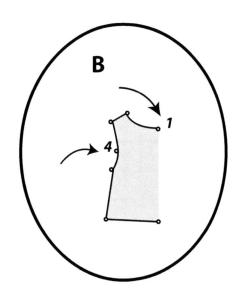

B

4

1

USE CENTER FRONT LINE TO GUIDE YOU

BASIC TANK TOP / INFANTS

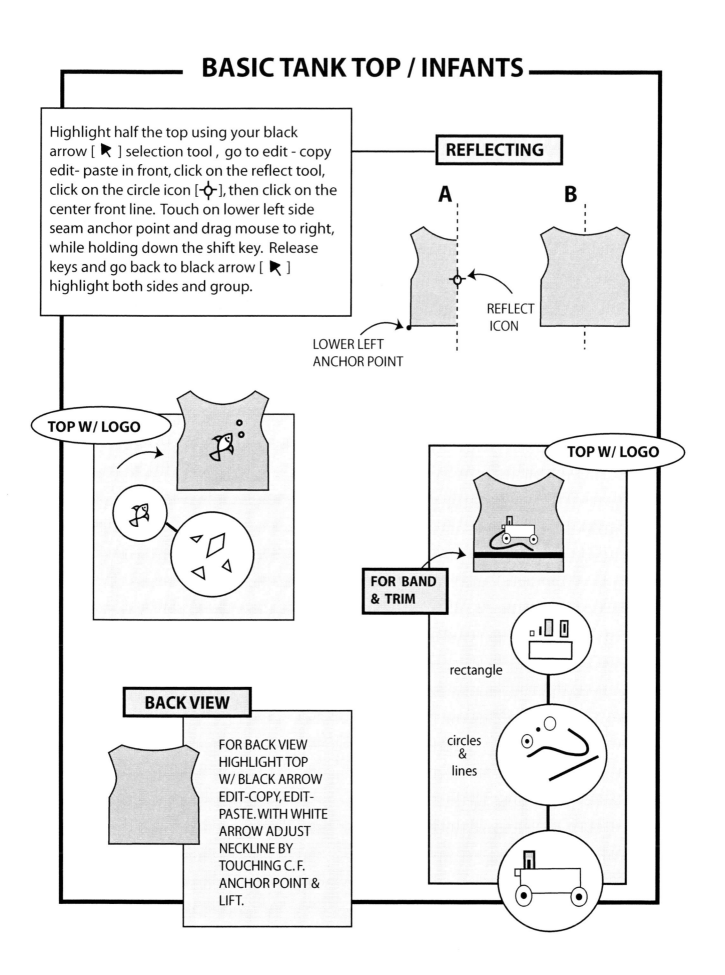

Highlight half the top using your black arrow [➤] selection tool , go to edit - copy edit- paste in front, click on the reflect tool, click on the circle icon [-◇-], then click on the center front line. Touch on lower left side seam anchor point and drag mouse to right, while holding down the shift key. Release keys and go back to black arrow [➤] highlight both sides and group.

REFLECTING

A   **B**

REFLECT ICON

LOWER LEFT ANCHOR POINT

TOP W/ LOGO

TOP W/ LOGO

FOR BAND & TRIM

rectangle

circles & lines

BACK VIEW

FOR BACK VIEW HIGHLIGHT TOP W/ BLACK ARROW EDIT-COPY, EDIT-PASTE. WITH WHITE ARROW ADJUST NECKLINE BY TOUCHING C.F. ANCHOR POINT & LIFT.

WORK SHEET
for RIBBING

RIBBING

To draw a ribbed neckline, start by drawing your neckline first. Place anchor point **1** on the center front line, anchor point **2** on shoulder line, anchor point **3** the width of the ribbing, and anchor point **4** back to C.F.

Using the convert direction point tool [⊾] on anchor point **1** and **4** curve the neckline to desired shape.

Add 4 small stroke lines starting from center front, copy & paste to add more of these to the neckline. Continue to add rib lines, once this is done, highlight the neckline and ribbing with the selection tool [⊾] and group.

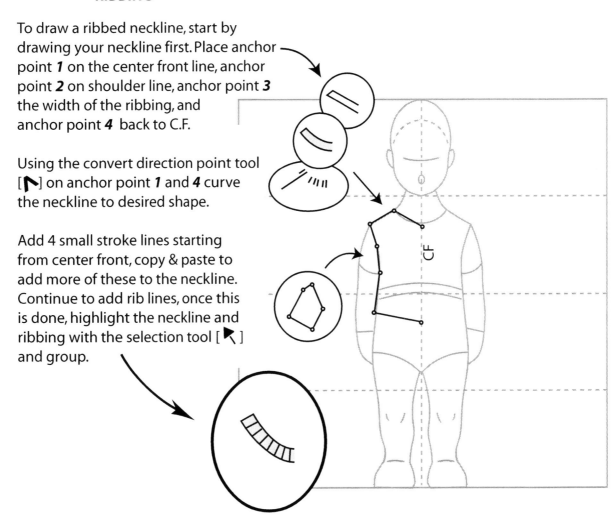

USE CENTER FRONT LINE TO GUIDE YOU,
KEEPING THE LOCATION OF DETAILS AND TRIM EVEN FROM C.F.

INFANTS
TOPS W/ RIBBING

BOYS TOP W/
FIRE ENGINE
APPLIQUE

GIRLS TOP
W/ FLOWER
APPLIQUE &
RUFFLE HEM

ENGINE CO. 1

WORKSHEET FOR
TOP W/SLEEVE

using 8 anchor points
for short sleeve....note
over lap of sleeve on bodice.

After 1/2 the top is done.....
Start your sleeve by placing anchor
point *1* on the inside shoulder line
(over lap armhole), as pictured to the
right. Place anchor point *2* at shoulder cap,
anchor point *3* touching arm for hem length,
anchor point *4* inside hemline, anchor point
5 at side seam of bodice, and anchor points
6,7,8 overlapping bodice armhole.

Using the convert direction point tool [➤],
drag anchor point *2* at shoulder cap to stretch
to the desired curve, and shape.

Highlight sleeve using your black arrow,
selection tool [➤], object - arrange - send to back.
Adjust the lower part of the sleeve to fit into the
armhole by dragging and lifting anchor point *5*
with the white arrow, direct selection tool [➤] to fit.
You can make many adjustments using your direct
selection tool [➤]. Use this tool to select open
anchor points and stretch.

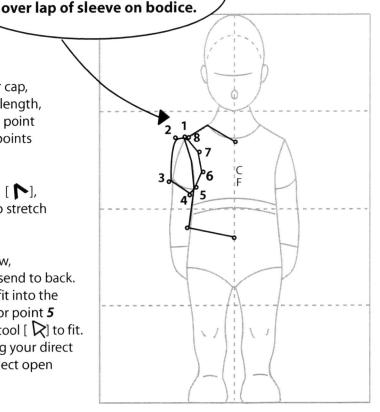

REFLECTING

Highlight half of the garment w/ black
arrow, selection tool [➤], go to edit -
copy -edit - paste in front. Highlight the
reflect tool [✦] and move the circle icon
[⬚] to the center front (C.F.). Touch on
the lower left side seam anchor point, click
and drag to right while holding down shift
key.....release keys and go back to black arrow.
Highlight both sides and group.

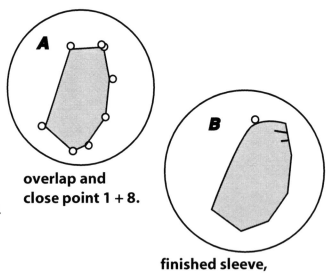

A

overlap and
close point 1 + 8.

B

finished sleeve,
w / shoulder curved.

INFANTS TOP
W/ SLEEVE

TUCKS FOR FULLNESS

BACK BUTTONS

FISH APPLIQUE

WORK SHEET for
LONG SLEEVE TOP

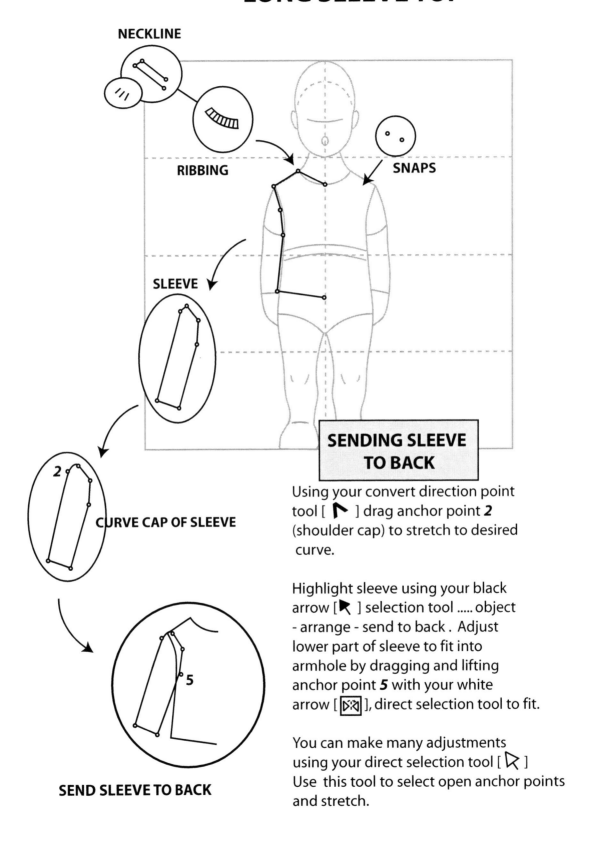

NECKLINE

RIBBING

SLEEVE

SNAPS

CURVE CAP OF SLEEVE

2

SEND SLEEVE TO BACK

5

SENDING SLEEVE TO BACK

Using your convert direction point tool [↖] drag anchor point **2** (shoulder cap) to stretch to desired curve.

Highlight sleeve using your black arrow [↖] selection tool ..... object - arrange - send to back . Adjust lower part of sleeve to fit into armhole by dragging and lifting anchor point **5** with your white arrow [⌧], direct selection tool to fit.

You can make many adjustments using your direct selection tool [↘] Use this tool to select open anchor points and stretch.

TOP W/ LONG SLEEVES & SHOULDER SNAPS

RIBBED NECKLINE
W/ SHOULDER SNAPS

WORK SHEET for
SHORT BODY SUIT

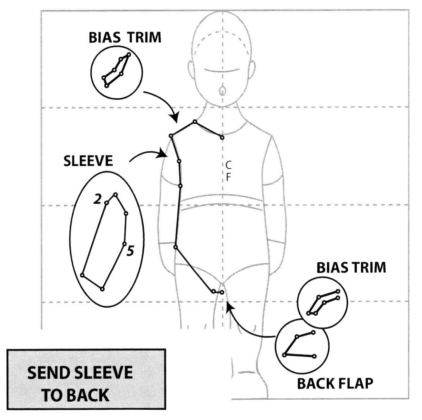

SEND SLEEVE TO BACK

Using your convert anchor point tool [↰], drag anchor point **2** (shoulder cap) to stretch to desired curve.

Highlight sleeve using your black arrow [◤] selection tool ..... object - arrange - send to back. Adjust lower part of sleeve to fit into armhole by dragging and lifting anchor point **5** with your white arrow [◸] direct selection tool to fit.

SHORT BODYSUIT

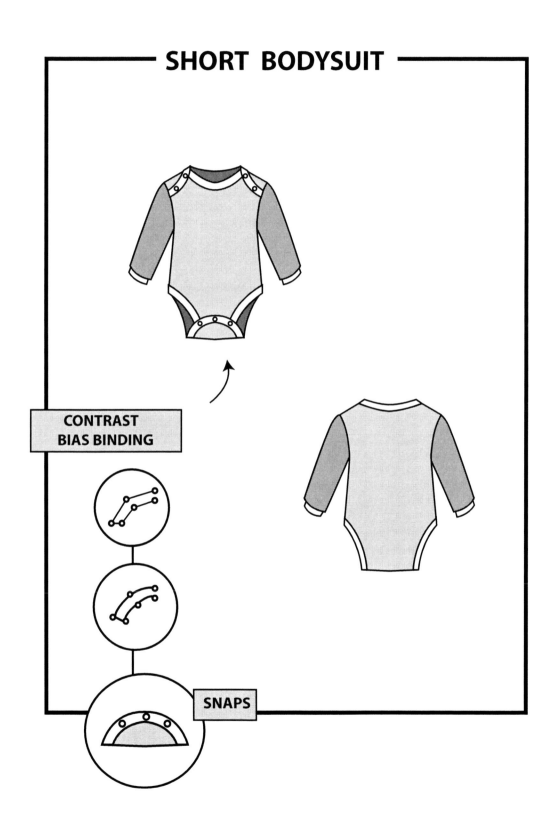

CONTRAST
BIAS BINDING

SNAPS

WORK SHEET for
LONG SLEEVE BODY SUIT

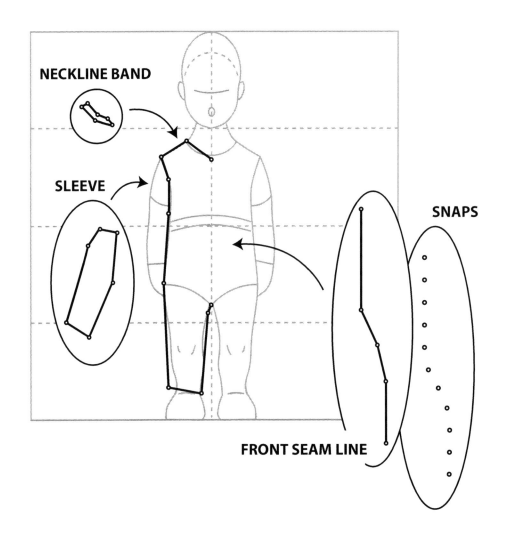

NECKLINE BAND

SLEEVE

SNAPS

FRONT SEAM LINE

LONG SLEEVE BODY SUIT

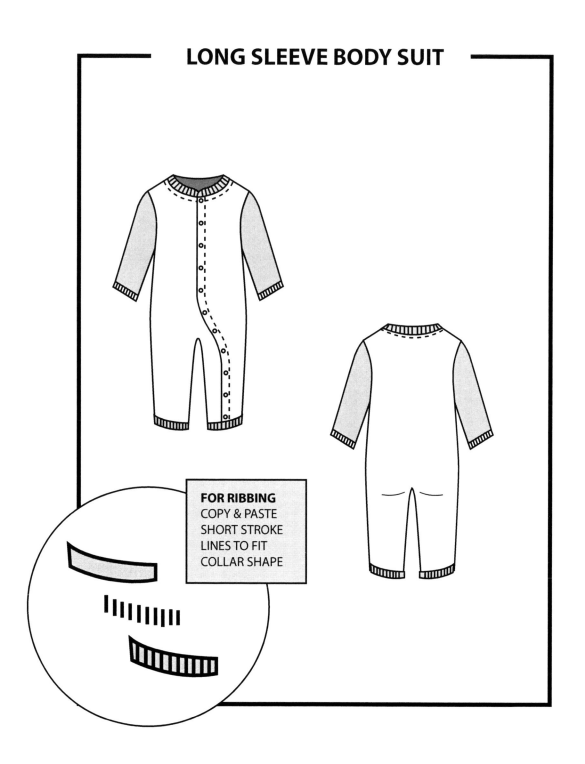

FOR RIBBING
COPY & PASTE
SHORT STROKE
LINES TO FIT
COLLAR SHAPE

WORK SHEET
for SHORT

FLAT WAISTBAND

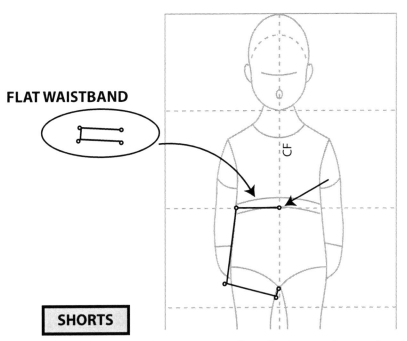

SHORTS

Start w/ your pen tool ....placing anchor point **1** on C.F. at waistline, as pictured above. Anchor point **2** at side of waist, anchor point **3** at the outside hemline, anchor point **4** inside hem, anchor point **5** on to the center front line of croqui. Make sure your top and bottom C.F. lines are in alignment before you reflect .

FLAT WAISTBAND

Add waistband by placing anchor point **1** w/ pen tool on C.F. above waistline, anchor point **2** at side of waistline (keep this line straight), anchor point **3** below for the width of the band, add last anchor point **4** on C.F. line. Highlight w/ selection tool [➤] and drag onto short waistline. Highlight short and waistband before reflecting.

REFLECTING

Highlight half the short leg w/ waistband using your selection tool [➤], go to edit - copy, edit- paste in front, click on the reflect tool [⊠], place the circle icon [-◇-], on the center front line. Touch on lower left side seam anchor point, and drag the mouse to right, holding down the shift key at the same time.....release keys and go back to the selection tool [➤], highlight both pieces and group.

INFANTS SHORTS W/ PATCH POCKETS

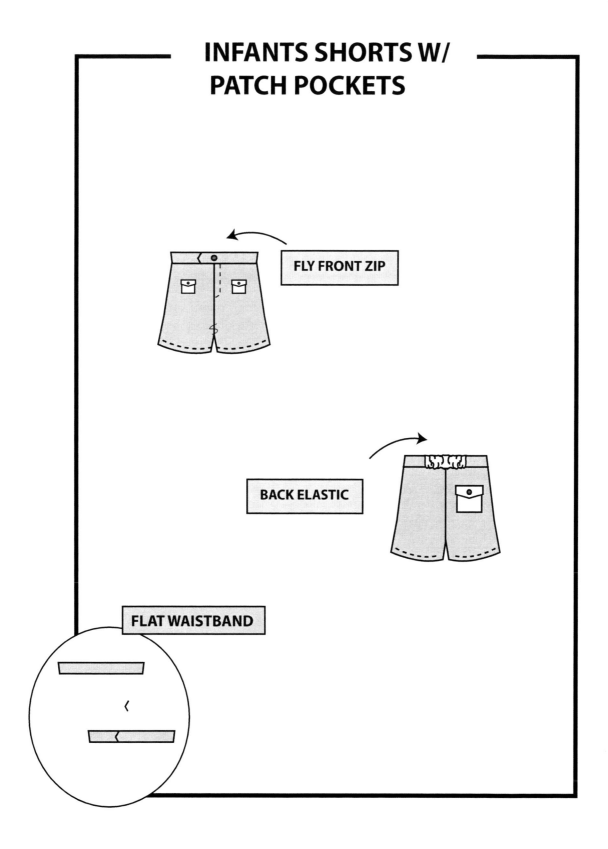

FLY FRONT ZIP

BACK ELASTIC

FLAT WAISTBAND

WORK SHEET for
ELASTIC WAIST

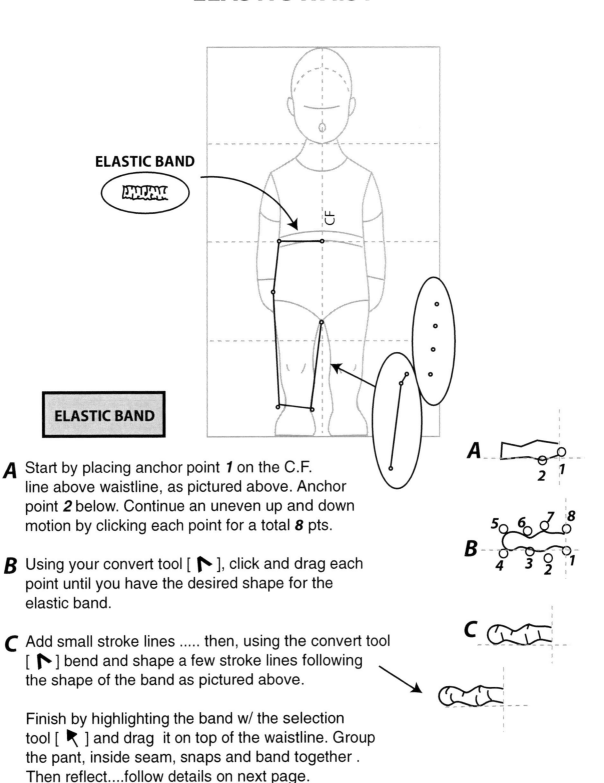

ELASTIC BAND

ELASTIC BAND

A Start by placing anchor point *1* on the C.F.
line above waistline, as pictured above. Anchor
point *2* below. Continue an uneven up and down
motion by clicking each point for a total *8* pts.

B Using your convert tool [↳], click and drag each
point until you have the desired shape for the
elastic band.

C Add small stroke lines ..... then, using the convert tool
[↳] bend and shape a few stroke lines following
the shape of the band as pictured above.

Finish by highlighting the band w/ the selection
tool [↖] and drag it on top of the waistline. Group
the pant, inside seam, snaps and band together .
Then reflect....follow details on next page.

BASIC PANTS W/ ELASTIC WAIST

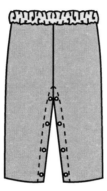
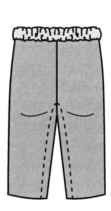

REFLECTING

Highlight half the pant leg using your black arrow [▶] selection tool, go to edit - copy edit- paste in front, click on the reflect tool [⊠] place the circle icon [⟡], on the center front line. Touch on lower left side seam anchor point and drag mouse to right holding down the shift key at the same time ..... release keys and go back to back arrow [▶], highlight both sides and group.

FRONT SEAM

Add front seam line by placing anchor point *1* on the c.f. line just below waistband, then place anchor point *2* touching c.f. crotch, where pant legs come together. Make sure you are using only the stroke line and fill is off.

WORK SHEET

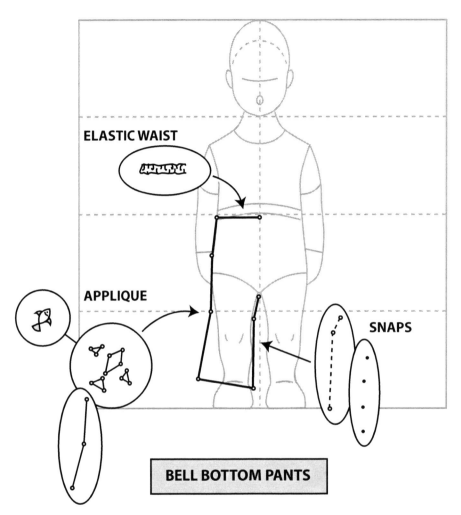

ELASTIC WAIST

APPLIQUE

SNAPS

BELL BOTTOM PANTS

A Start w/ your pen tool ....place anchor point *1* on C.F. at waistline, as pictured above. Anchor point *2* at the side of the waist, anchor point *3* at hip line, anchor point *4* above the knee , anchor point *5* outside hemline, anchor point *6* inside hem, anchor point *7* above the knee and anchor point *8* at the center front line of the croqui.
Make sure your top and bottom C.F. lines are in alignment before you reflect .

B Using your convert direction point tool [↰] drag open anchor pt. *4* and *7* up or down to get smooth curve for bell shape pant.

INFANT BELL PANTS
W/ APPLIQUE

ELASTIC WAIST

CREATE NEW PANT DESIGNS BY USING

OTHER DETAILS AND TRIM.

WORK SHEET for
OVERALL

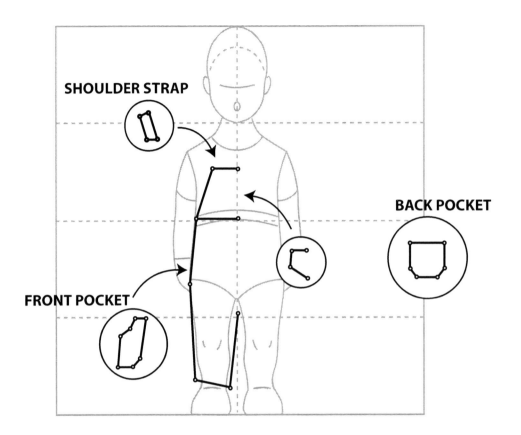

SHOULDER STRAP

BACK POCKET

FRONT POCKET

INFANT OVERALL

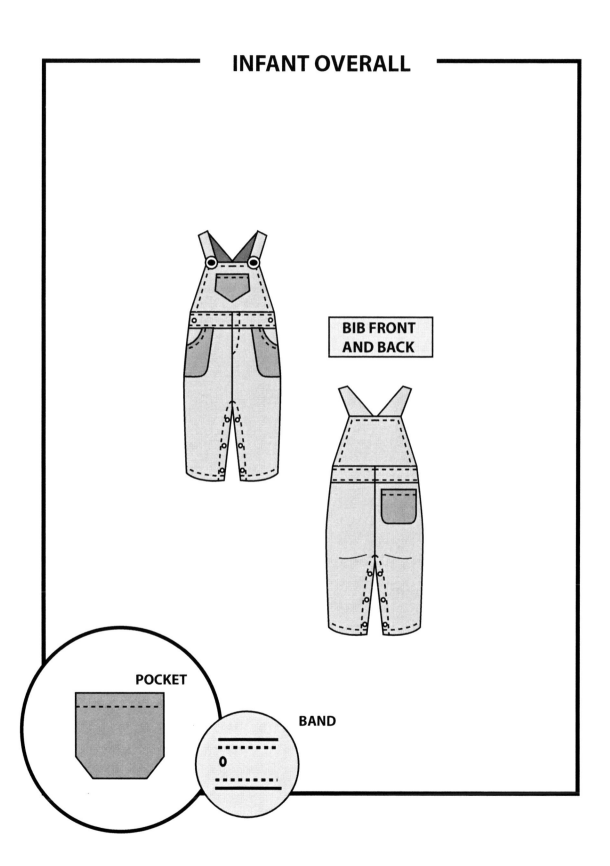

BIB FRONT
AND BACK

POCKET

BAND

0

83

WORK SHEET
for DRESS

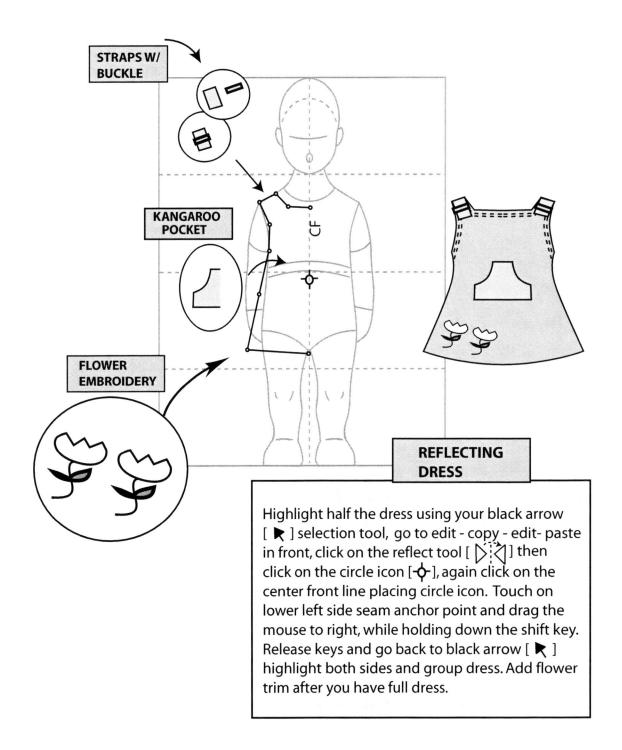

STRAPS W/ BUCKLE

KANGAROO POCKET

CF

FLOWER EMBROIDERY

REFLECTING DRESS

Highlight half the dress using your black arrow [▶] selection tool, go to edit - copy - edit- paste in front, click on the reflect tool [▷◁] then click on the circle icon [-◇-], again click on the center front line placing circle icon. Touch on lower left side seam anchor point and drag the mouse to right, while holding down the shift key. Release keys and go back to black arrow [▶] highlight both sides and group dress. Add flower trim after you have full dress.

DRESSES

FOR FLOWER DESIGN...USE 6 CIRCLES AROUND 1 LARGE CONTRAST CIRCLE.

FOR APRON DESIGN USE THIS SHAPE 1ST, THEN DRAW RUFFLE. FOR BAND USE A POINT 2 STROKE LINE FOR THIS EFFECT.

FOR EMBROIDERY DESIGN USE 4 CIRCLES WITH CONTRAST SMALL CIRCLE ON CENTER. FOR LEAF USE PENCIL TOOL.

INFANTS A-LINE SKIRT

FLY FRONT ZIP W/ PATCH POCKETS

BACK ELASTIC

FISH APPLIQUE W/ TOP STITCH HEMLINE

INFANTS GATHERED
SKIRT W/ BIB FRONT

BIB W/ FLOWER APPLIQUE & TOP STITCHING

PATCH POCKETS & BUTTON FRONT

SHOULDER STRAPS

BACK ELASTIC

WORK SHEET

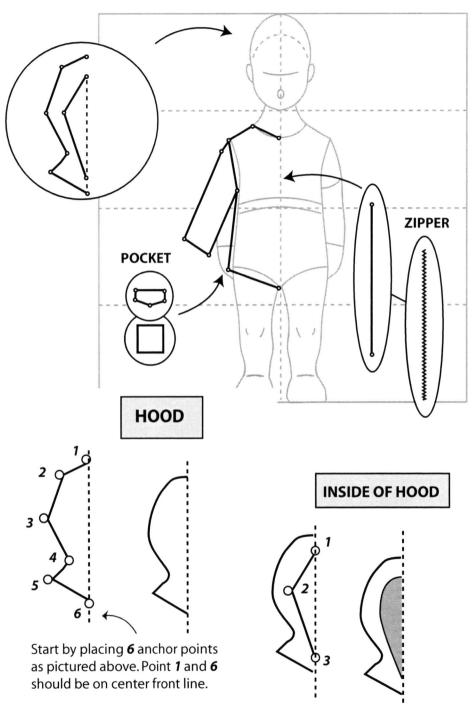

POCKET

ZIPPER

HOOD

Start by placing **6** anchor points as pictured above. Point **1** and **6** should be on center front line.

Curve anchor points. Drag anchor point **1** to the right or left, **2**, **3** and drag **4** down.

INSIDE OF HOOD

Start with anchor point **1** on C.F. Anchor point **2** inside hood and ancor point **3** on C.F. Curve points **1** and **2** to desired shape. Send hood to the back. Reflect the whole garment. Add seamline to the hood before completing.

JACKET W/ HOOD

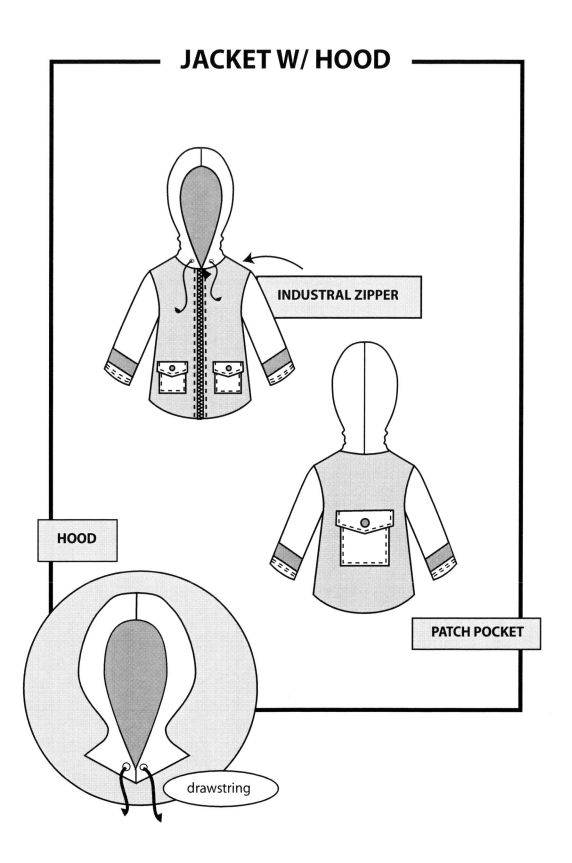

INDUSTRAL ZIPPER

HOOD

PATCH POCKET

drawstring

INFANT
INDUSTRIAL ZIPPERS

Draw a straight line with the pen tool.

Make sure the fill is *OFF* and *STROKE* line is *ON*.

Highlight with the selection tool.

Go to **FILTER - DISTORT- ZIG ZAG**
OPTIONS - SIZE 1
RELATIVE - RIDGES PER SEGMENT 30
(this size will depend on the length of your zipper)
POINTS - CORNER

This method can be used to show an industrial zipper on jackets and sweat shirts with hoods. By practicing these steps several times you will be able to create new looks with zippers.

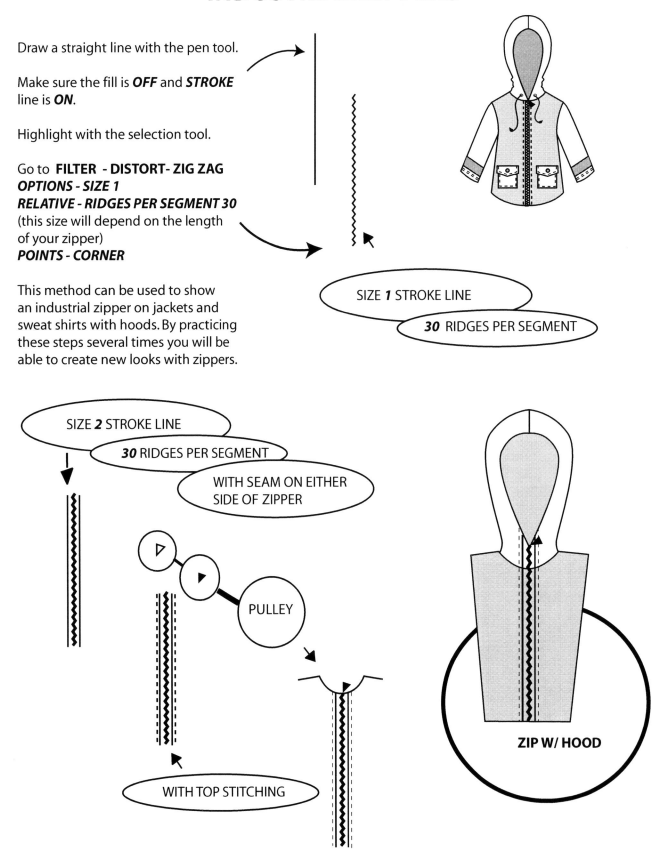

SIZE *1* STROKE LINE

30 RIDGES PER SEGMENT

SIZE *2* STROKE LINE

30 RIDGES PER SEGMENT

WITH SEAM ON EITHER SIDE OF ZIPPER

PULLEY

WITH TOP STITCHING

ZIP W/ HOOD

TOPS W/ ZIPPERS

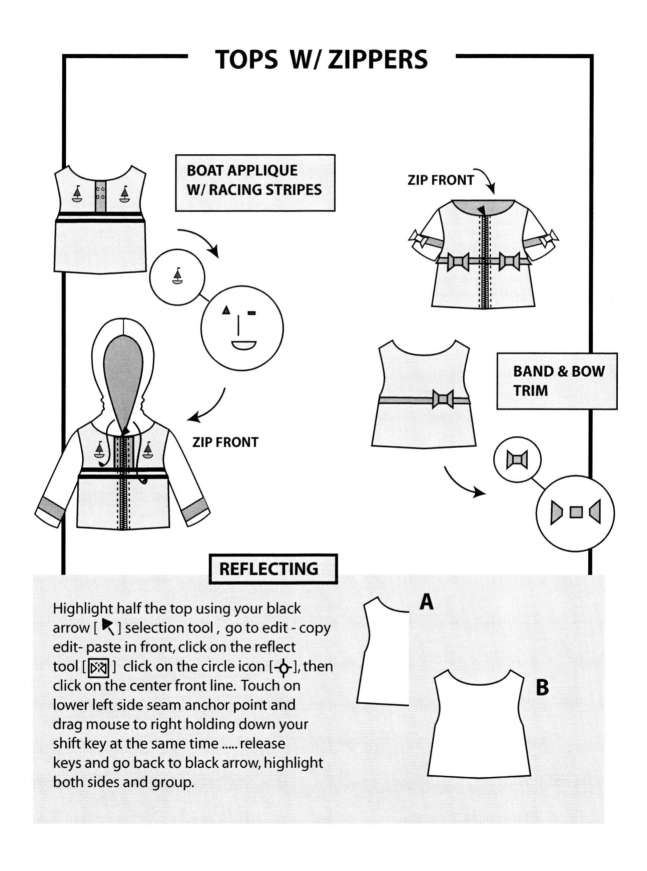

BOAT APPLIQUE W/ RACING STRIPES

ZIP FRONT

ZIP FRONT

BAND & BOW TRIM

REFLECTING

Highlight half the top using your black arrow [➤] selection tool , go to edit - copy edit- paste in front, click on the reflect tool [⊠] click on the circle icon [⬦], then click on the center front line. Touch on lower left side seam anchor point and drag mouse to right holding down your shift key at the same time ..... release keys and go back to black arrow, highlight both sides and group.

A

B

THE LOCATION OF DETAILS AND TRIM EVEN FROM C.F.

91

MENS WEAR

MEN - BACK CROQUI

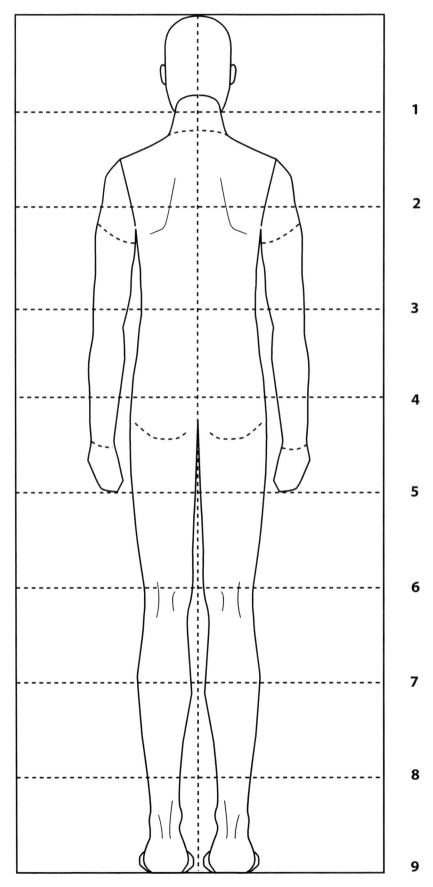

1

2

3

4

5

6

7

8

9

MEN - FRONT CROQUI

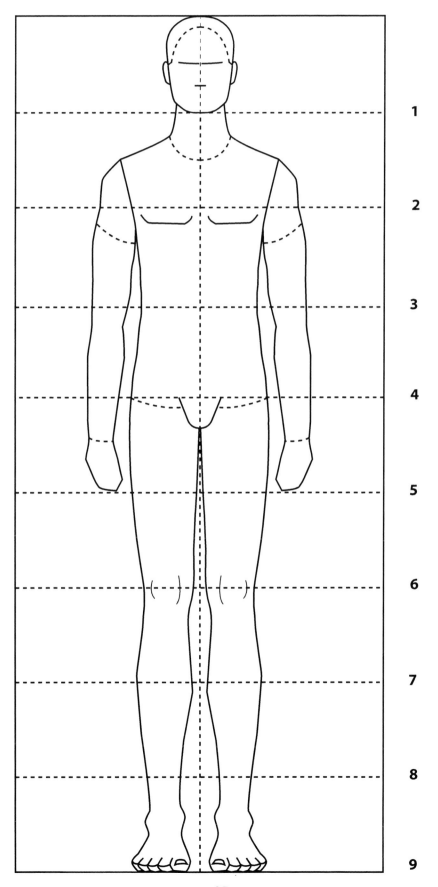

1

2

3

4

5

6

7

8

9

95

MEN'S TANK TOP WORKSHEET

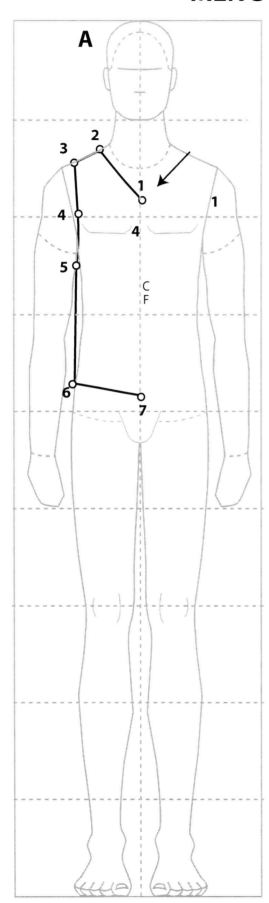

A

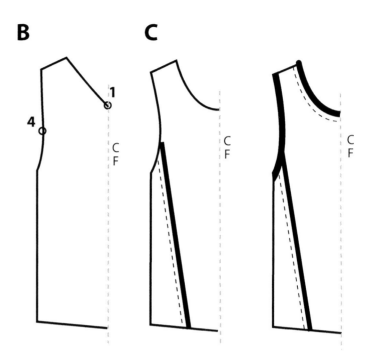

B   C

A Start w/ your pen tool ..... place anchor point *1* on C.F. at neckline as pictured above. Anchor point *2* at shoulder, anchor point *3* at shoulder/armhole, anchor point *4* inside armhole, anchor point *5* underarm , anchor point *6* at hip side seam and anchor point *7* at hemline, going back to C.F.

B Using your convert tool [ ] click and drag anchor point *1* to the left to get the shape of the neckline. Drag anchor point *4* down to get the shape of the armhole. Make sure your fill color is on! This makes the process of keeping your C.F. of the garment lined up w/ the dotted line of the croqui. Finish all details on one side before reflecting your top.

Using your white arrow [ ] highlight only the open anchor points you want to change. You can do the same process to shape the top, drop the neckline and shorten or lengthen the hemline.

C This is the shape of the neckline and armhole you would want before reflecting. You can develop the design with added detail after practicing these simple steps several times. There are many ways of developing new styles using this program. Add piping 1st; then armhole band, last neckline (note the different size stroke lines).

96

MEN'S TANK W/CONTRAST BAND

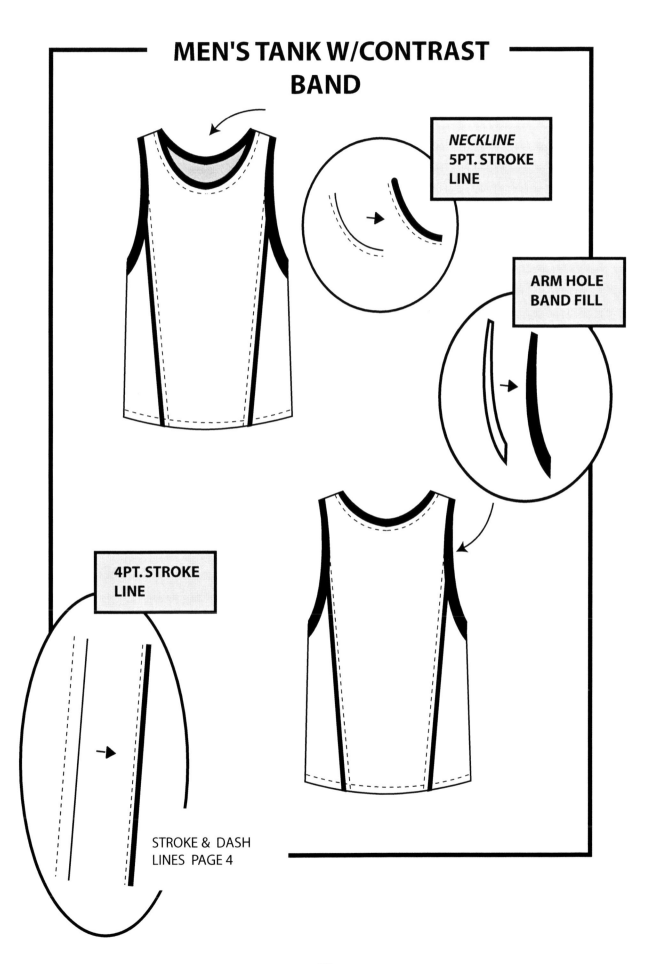

NECKLINE
5PT. STROKE
LINE

ARM HOLE
BAND FILL

4PT. STROKE
LINE

STROKE & DASH
LINES PAGE 4

WORKSHEET FOR JEAN STYLE

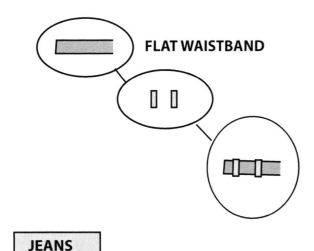

FLAT WAISTBAND

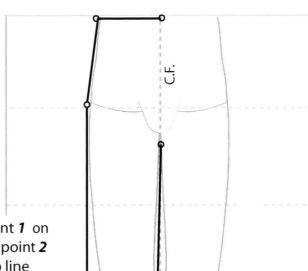

C.F.

Start w/ your pen tool ..... place anchor point **1** on C.F. at waistline as pictured above. Anchor point **2** at side of waist , anchor point **3** outside hip line anchor point **4** outside hem, anchor point **5** inside hem and anchor point **6** on C.F. crotch line. Make sure your top and bottom C.F. lines are in alignment before reflecting .

FLAT WAISTBAND

Add waistband by placing anchor point **1** w/ pen tool on C.F. above waistline, anchor point **2** at side of waistline (keep this line straight), anchor point **3** below for width of band, add last anchor point **4** on C.F. line. Highlight w/ selection tool [➤] and drag onto pant waistline. Highlight pant and waistband before reflecting.

REFLECTING

Highlight half the pant leg w/ waistband using your black arrow [➤] selection tool , go to edit - copy edit- paste in front, click on the reflect tool [⊠] place the circle icon [⟡], on the center front line. Touch on lower left side seam anchor point, and drag mouse to right, holding down the shift key at the same time ..... release keys and go back to black arrow, [➤] highlight both pieces and group.

JEANS

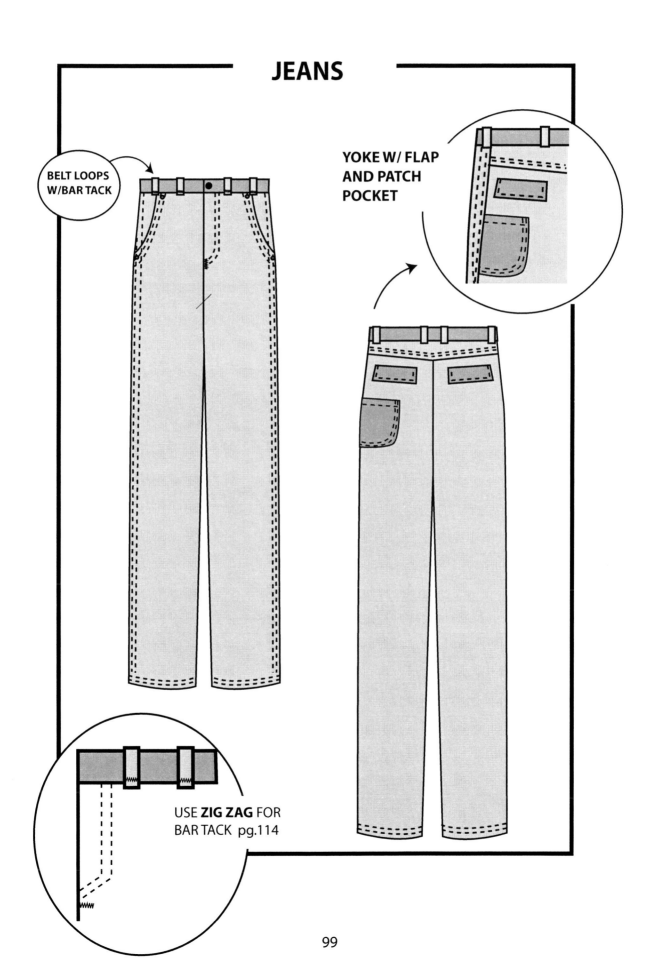

BELT LOOPS
W/ BAR TACK

YOKE W/ FLAP
AND PATCH
POCKET

USE **ZIG ZAG** FOR
BAR TACK pg.114

WORKSHEET FOR CARGO PANT

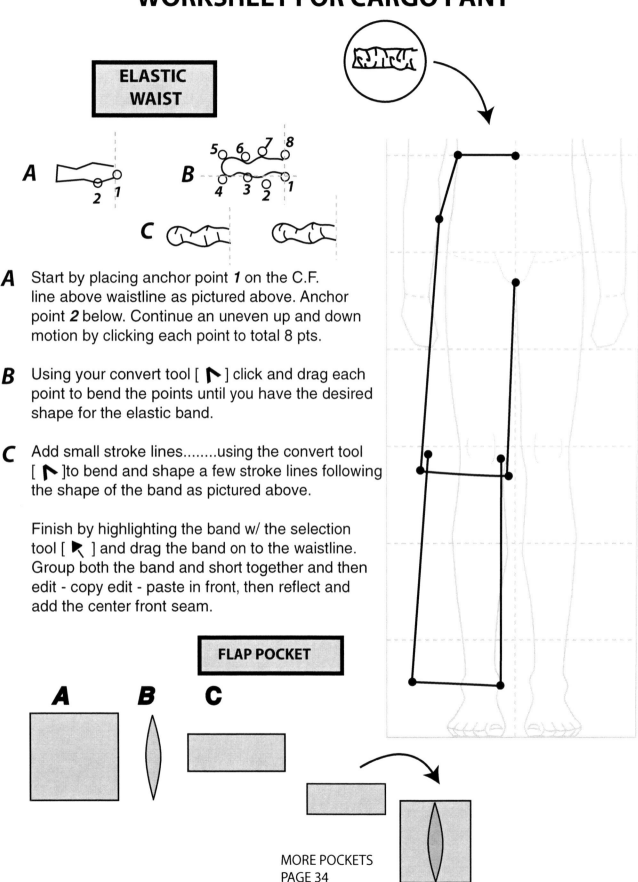

ELASTIC WAIST

A

B

C

A Start by placing anchor point *1* on the C.F. line above waistline as pictured above. Anchor point *2* below. Continue an uneven up and down motion by clicking each point to total 8 pts.

B Using your convert tool [↖] click and drag each point to bend the points until you have the desired shape for the elastic band.

C Add small stroke lines........using the convert tool [↖]to bend and shape a few stroke lines following the shape of the band as pictured above.

Finish by highlighting the band w/ the selection tool [↖] and drag the band on to the waistline. Group both the band and short together and then edit - copy edit - paste in front, then reflect and add the center front seam.

FLAP POCKET

A   *B*   *C*

MORE POCKETS
PAGE 34

100

CARGO PANTS

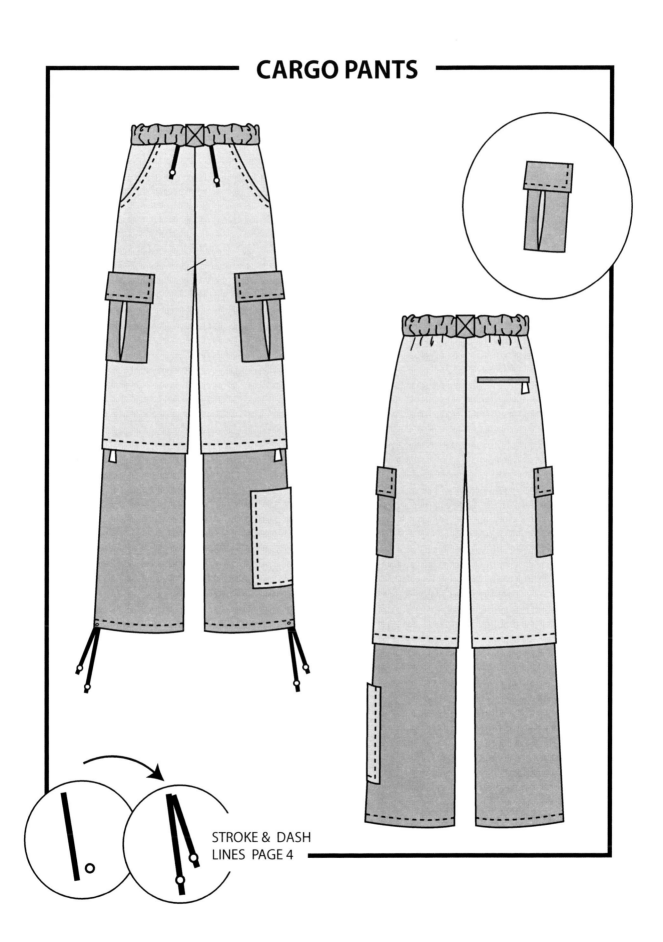

STROKE & DASH
LINES PAGE 4

MEN'S T-SHIRT WORKSHEET

RIBBING

To draw a ribbed neckline, start by drawing the neckline first. Place Anchor point *1* on the center front line, anchor point *2* on shoulder line, anchor point *3* at the width of the ribbing, and anchor point *4* back to C.F.

Using the convert, direction point tool [⌐] on anchor points *1* and *4* curve the neckline to desired shape.

Add 4 small stroke lines starting from center front, copy & paste, add these to neckline. Continue to add rib lines. Once this is done highlight neckline and ribbing with [⌐] selection tool and group. These stroke lines can be any amount that work for the image . Highlight and group all parts of shirt and reflect.

RIB NECKLINE

RIB CUFF

RIB HEM

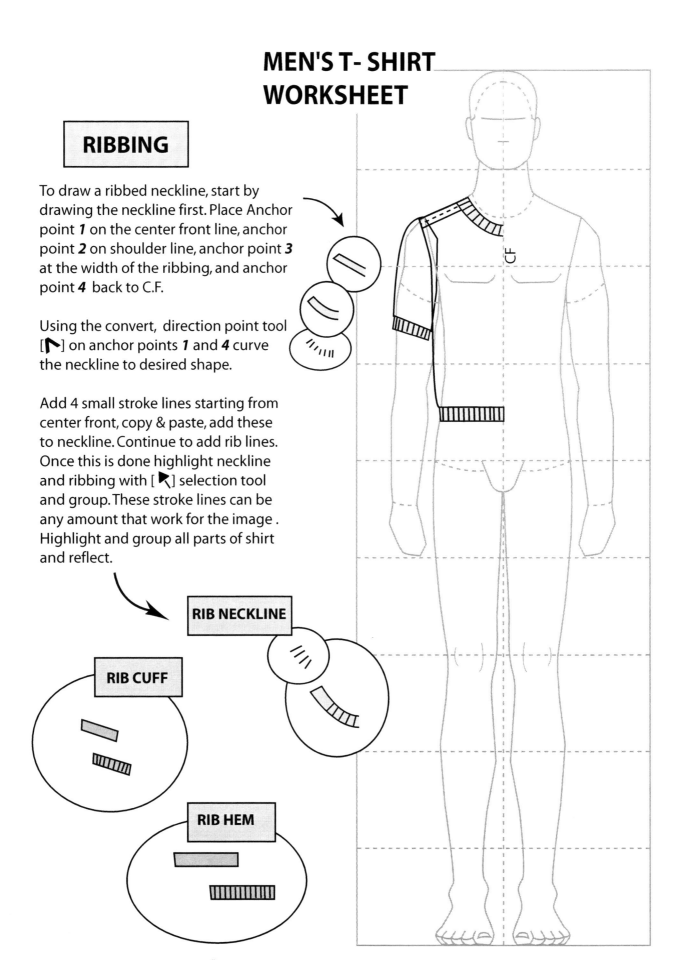

T - SHIRTS W/ RIBBING

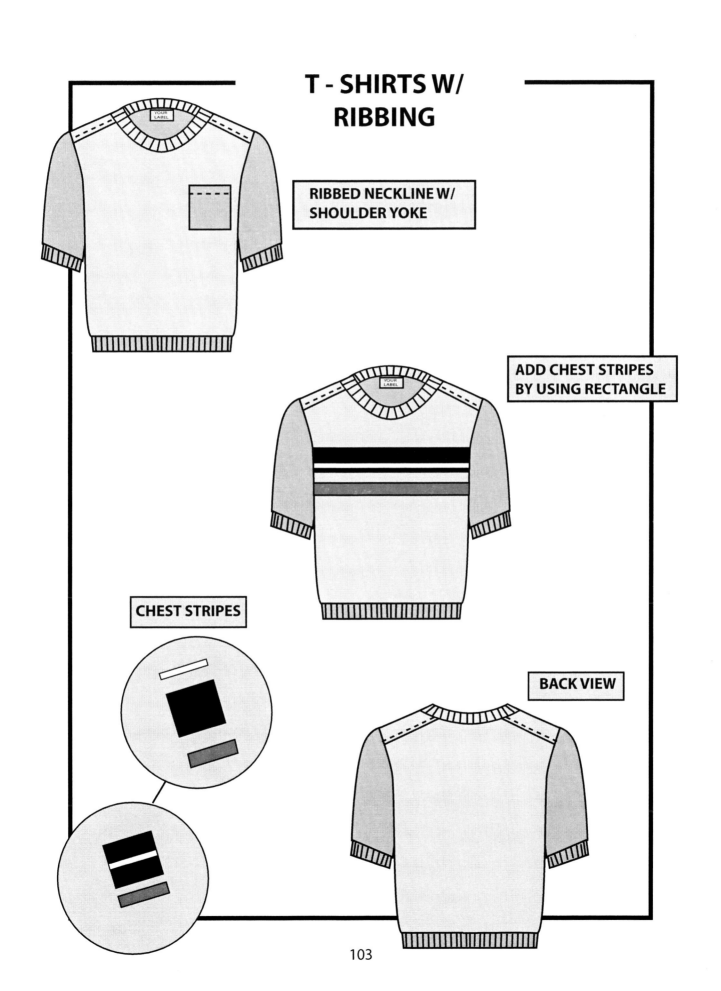

RIBBED NECKLINE W/ SHOULDER YOKE

ADD CHEST STRIPES BY USING RECTANGLE

CHEST STRIPES

BACK VIEW

YOUR LABEL

POLO SHIRT
WORKSHEET

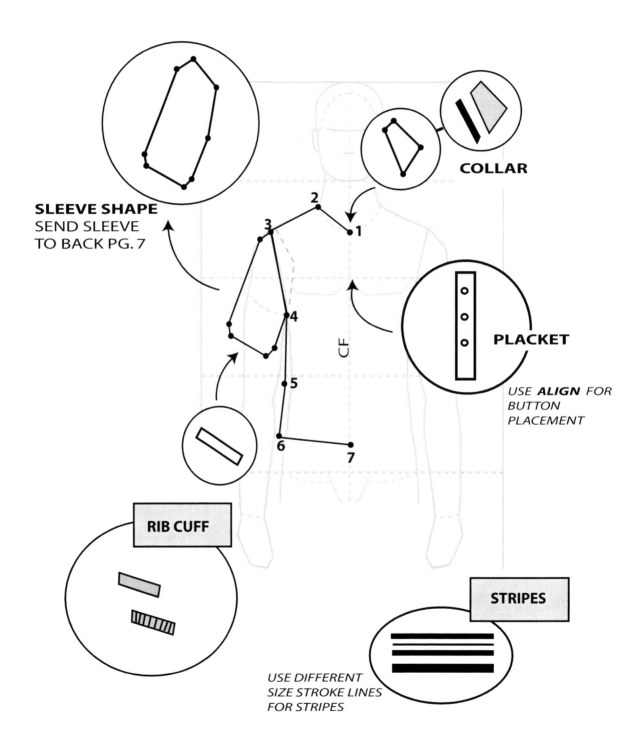

SLEEVE SHAPE
SEND SLEEVE
TO BACK PG. 7

COLLAR

PLACKET

*USE **ALIGN** FOR
BUTTON
PLACEMENT*

CF

2

3

1

4

5

6

7

RIB CUFF

STRIPES

*USE DIFFERENT
SIZE STROKE LINES
FOR STRIPES*

STROKE AND DASH
LINES PAGE 4

POLO SHIRT W/ CHEST STRIPES

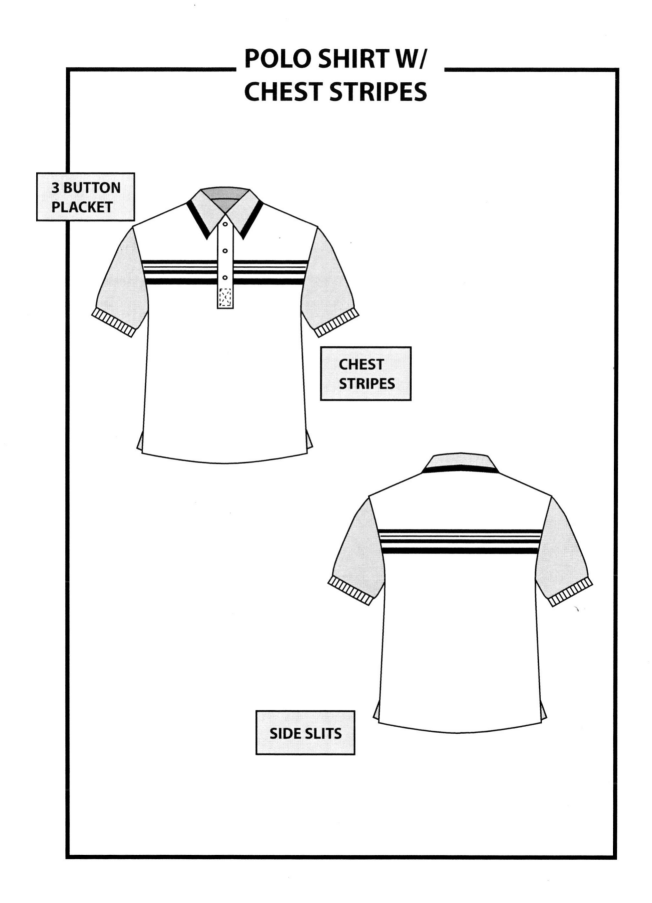

3 BUTTON PLACKET

CHEST STRIPES

SIDE SLITS

CABANA WORK SHEET

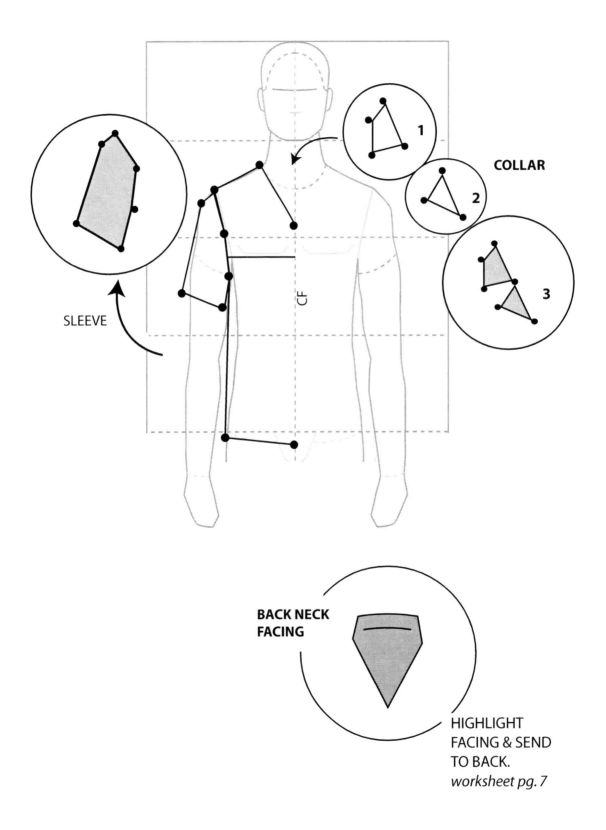

SLEEVE

COLLAR

1

2

3

CF

BACK NECK FACING

HIGHLIGHT
FACING & SEND
TO BACK.
worksheet pg. 7

CABANA SHIRT

YOKE WITH TOP STITCH

STRIPES

WESTERN SHIRT WORKSHEET

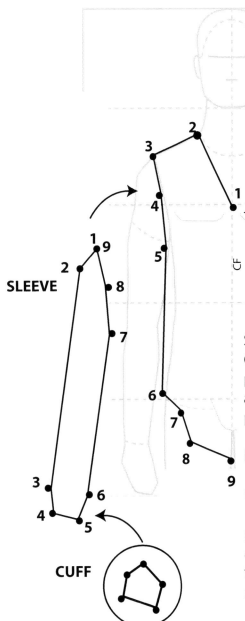

COLLAR

SLEEVE

CUFF

SLEEVE & CUFF
Sleeve has **9** anchor points for this shape, close the sleeve with **9**th anchor point. Add cuff after sleeve is finished. Drag onto shirt, then copy, paste-in front, and reflect.

Start w/ your pen tool ....place anchor point **1** on C.F. below neckline as pictured above. Anchor point **2** at shoulder, anchor point **3** at shoulder/ armhole, anchor point **4** inside armhole, anchor point **5** underarm, anchor point **6** at hip side seam anchor point **7** at hip curve, anchor point **8** at lower hemline, and anchor point **9** going back to C.F.

Using your convert tool [✎] drag anchor point **1** to the left to get shape of neckline. Drag anchor point **4** down to get the shape of the armhole. Drag anchor points **7** and **8** to curve hem. Make sure your fill color is on! Finish all details on one side before reflecting your top.

Using your white arrow [▷] highlight only the open anchor points you want to change. You can do the same process to shape the top.....drop the neckline, shorten or lengthen the hemline.

This is the shape of the top with sleeve and cuff you would want before reflecting. You can develop the design with added detail .

WESTERN SHIRT

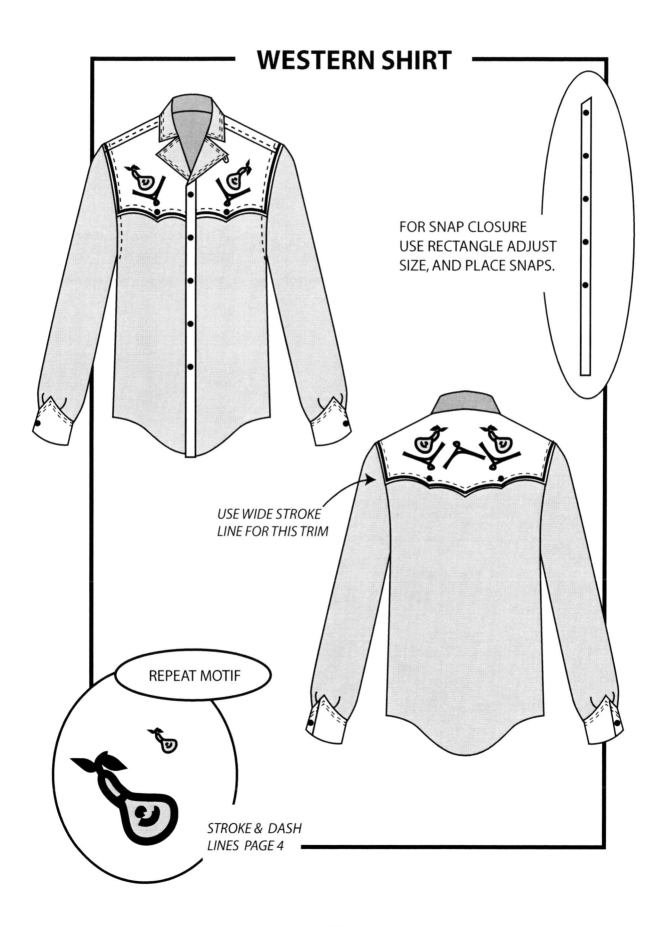

FOR SNAP CLOSURE
USE RECTANGLE ADJUST
SIZE, AND PLACE SNAPS.

*USE WIDE STROKE
LINE FOR THIS TRIM*

REPEAT MOTIF

*STROKE & DASH
LINES PAGE 4*

SINGLE BREASTED
JACKET WORKSHEET

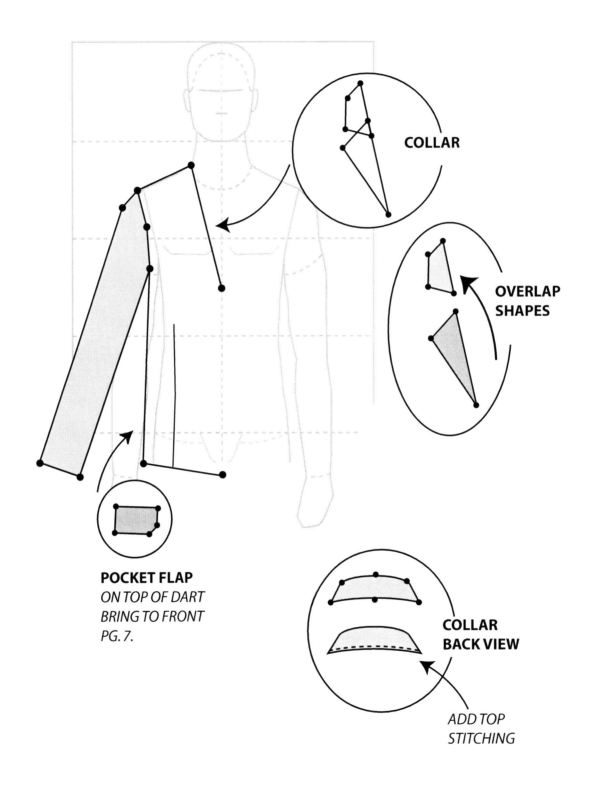

COLLAR

**OVERLAP
SHAPES**

POCKET FLAP
*ON TOP OF DART
BRING TO FRONT
PG. 7.*

**COLLAR
BACK VIEW**

*ADD TOP
STITCHING*

SINGLE BREASTED
JACKET

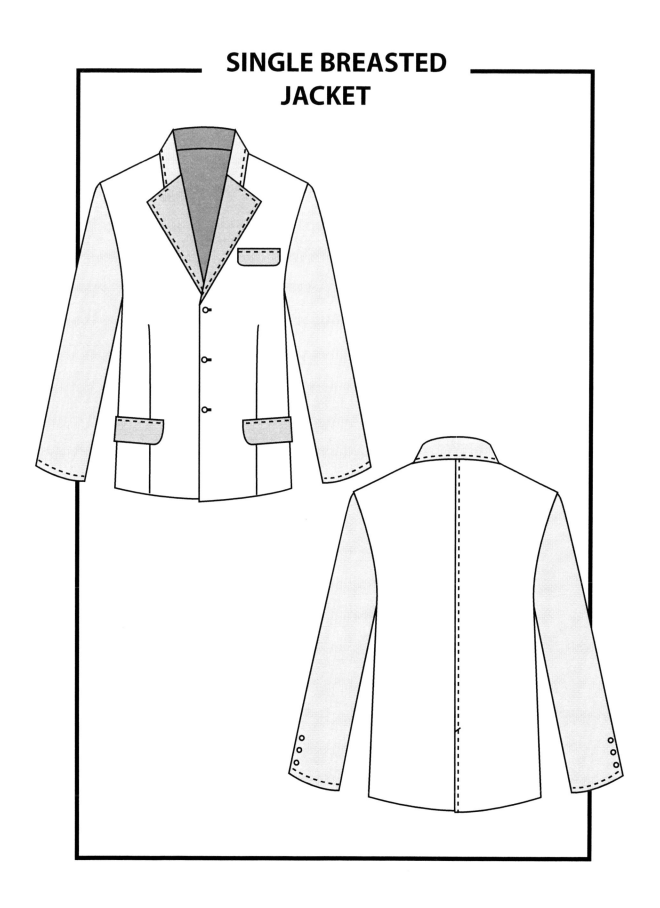

HOOD WORKSHEET

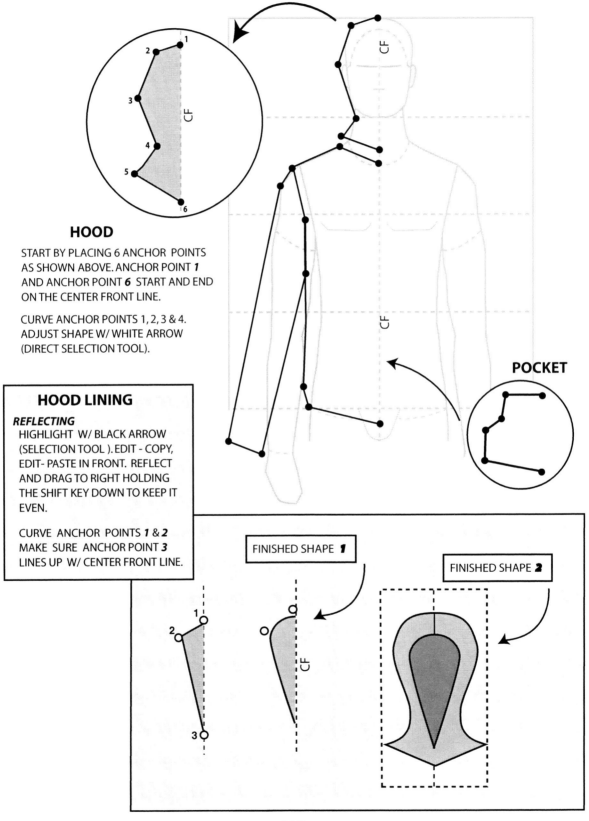

HOOD

START BY PLACING 6 ANCHOR POINTS AS SHOWN ABOVE. ANCHOR POINT **1** AND ANCHOR POINT **6** START AND END ON THE CENTER FRONT LINE.

CURVE ANCHOR POINTS 1, 2, 3 & 4. ADJUST SHAPE W/ WHITE ARROW (DIRECT SELECTION TOOL).

HOOD LINING

REFLECTING

HIGHLIGHT W/ BLACK ARROW (SELECTION TOOL). EDIT - COPY, EDIT- PASTE IN FRONT. REFLECT AND DRAG TO RIGHT HOLDING THE SHIFT KEY DOWN TO KEEP IT EVEN.

CURVE ANCHOR POINTS **1** & **2** MAKE SURE ANCHOR POINT **3** LINES UP W/ CENTER FRONT LINE.

POCKET

FINISHED SHAPE **1**

FINISHED SHAPE **2**

SWEATSHIRT W/ HOOD

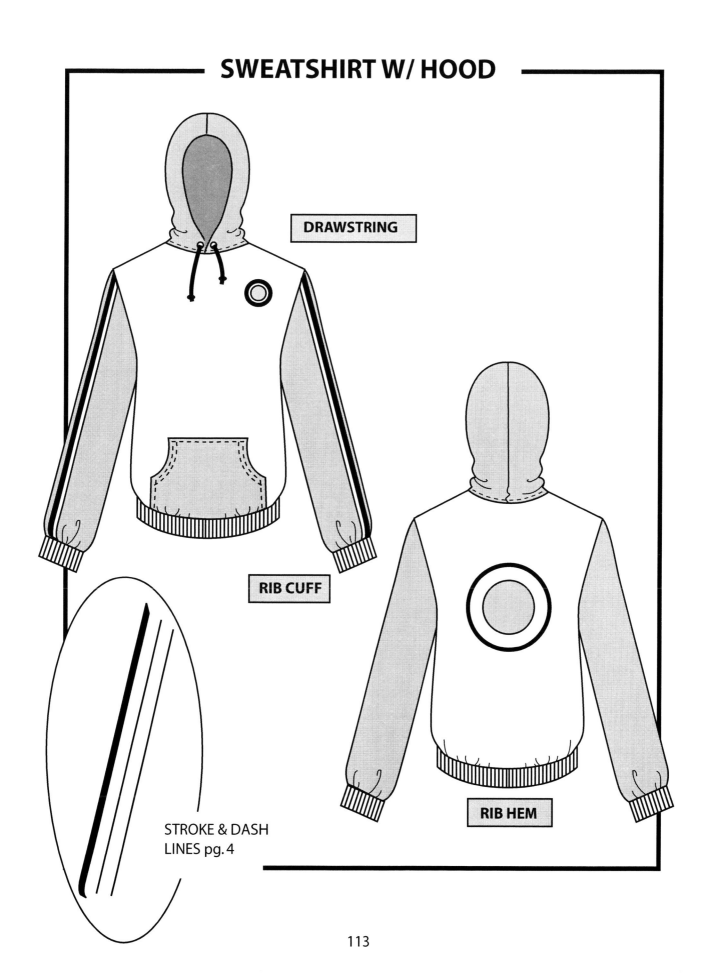

DRAWSTRING

RIB CUFF

STROKE & DASH
LINES pg. 4

RIB HEM

INDUSTRIAL ZIPPER WORKSHEET

Draw a straight line with the pen tool.

Make sure the fill is **OFF** and **STROKE** line is **ON**, as pictured to the right.

Highlight with selection tool.

Go to **FILTER - DISTORT- ZIG ZAG OPTIONS - SIZE 1 RELATIVE - RIDGES PER SEGMENT** 40 [this size will depend on the length of your zipper] **POINTS - CORNER**

This method can be used to show an industrial zipper on jackets, shorts sweat shirts and pants . By practicing these steps several times you will be able to create new details with zippers. This vest has a pocket w/ a zipper. Use the rectangle tool 1st, then drag zipper on top.

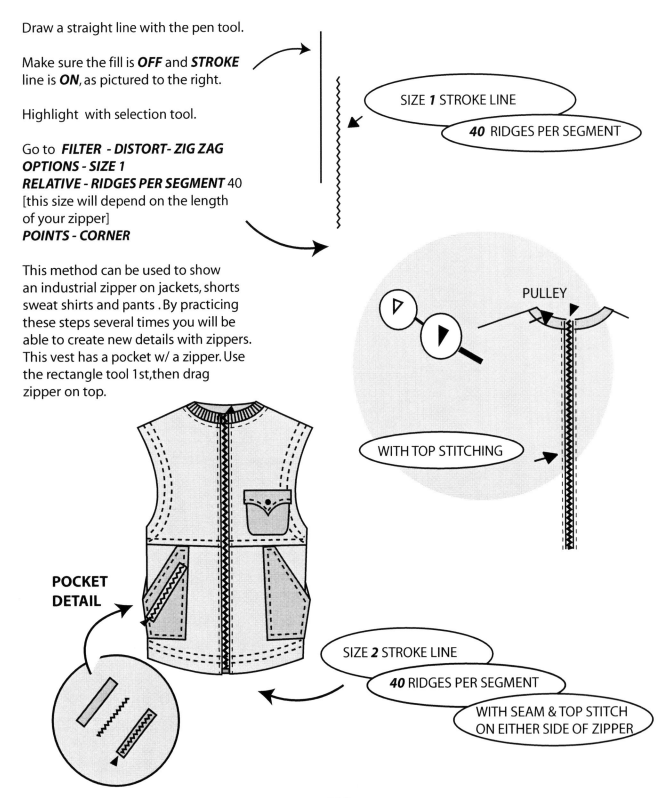

SIZE **1** STROKE LINE

40 RIDGES PER SEGMENT

PULLEY

WITH TOP STITCHING

POCKET DETAIL

SIZE **2** STROKE LINE

40 RIDGES PER SEGMENT

WITH SEAM & TOP STITCH ON EITHER SIDE OF ZIPPER

JOGGING PANT W/ RACING STRIPES

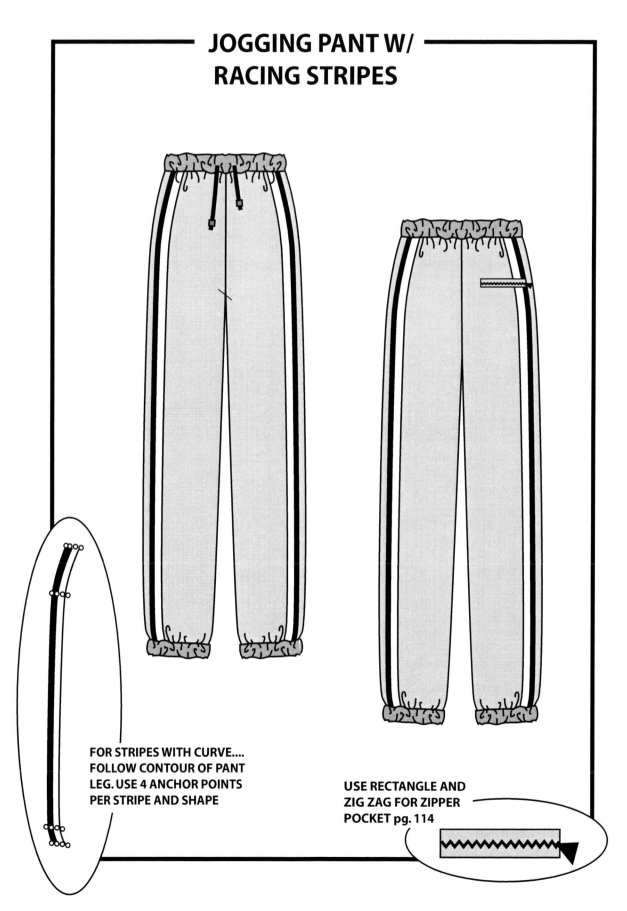

FOR STRIPES WITH CURVE....
FOLLOW CONTOUR OF PANT
LEG. USE 4 ANCHOR POINTS
PER STRIPE AND SHAPE

USE RECTANGLE AND
ZIG ZAG FOR ZIPPER
POCKET pg. 114

MEN'S DRESS PANT

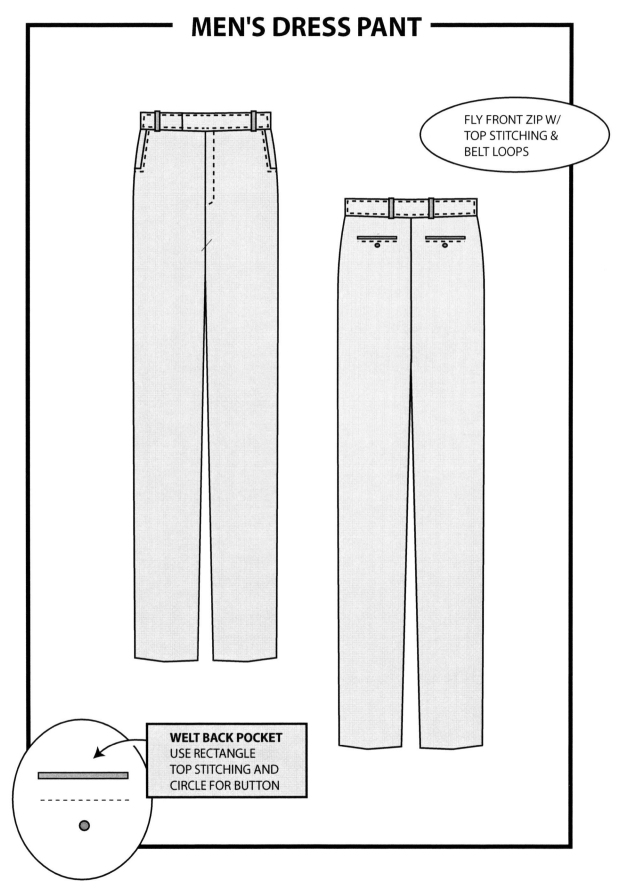

FLY FRONT ZIP W/
TOP STITCHING &
BELT LOOPS

WELT BACK POCKET
USE RECTANGLE
TOP STITCHING AND
CIRCLE FOR BUTTON

MEN'S DRESS PANT
W/CUFFS & TABS

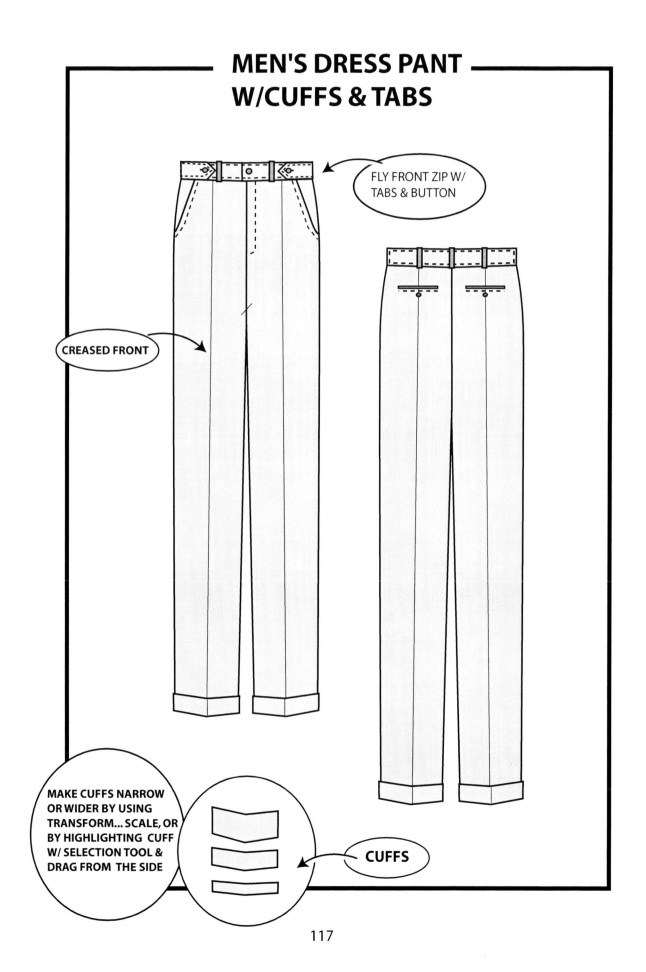

FLY FRONT ZIP W/ TABS & BUTTON

CREASED FRONT

MAKE CUFFS NARROW OR WIDER BY USING TRANSFORM... SCALE, OR BY HIGHLIGHTING CUFF W/ SELECTION TOOL & DRAG FROM THE SIDE

CUFFS

SHORTS

FLAT FRONT
SHORTS

BACK WELT
POCKET

SHORTS W/ CUFFS

BACK YOKE

USE RECTANGLE
TOOL FOR POCKET

MORE POCKETS pg.34

SHORTS

PLEATED SHORTS
W/ DRAWSTRING
WAIST

BACK VIEW W/
FLAP POCKETS

CARGO SHORTS
W/ ZIP OFF POCKETS

3/4 VIEW W/ BACK
FLAP & PATCH
POCKET

FOR ZIP USE
ZIG ZAG pg. 114

T - SHIRTS

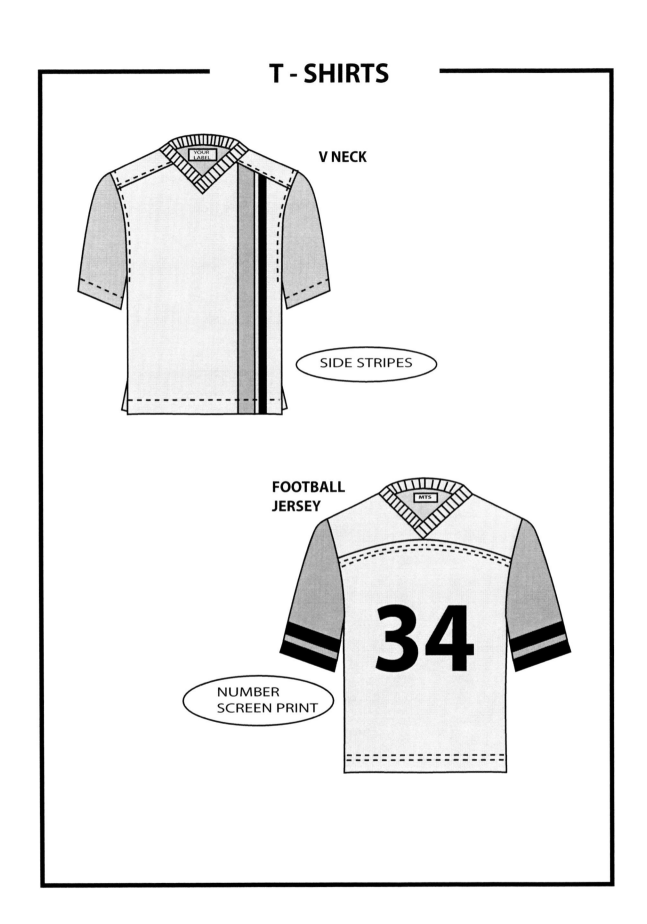

V NECK

YOUR LABEL

SIDE STRIPES

FOOTBALL
JERSEY

MTS

34

NUMBER
SCREEN PRINT

SHIRTS

POLO

YOUR LABEL

LONG BACK

PLACKET FRONT

YOUR LABEL

SIDE OPENING

121

BANDED COLLAR
SHIRT

MEN'S DRESS SHIRT

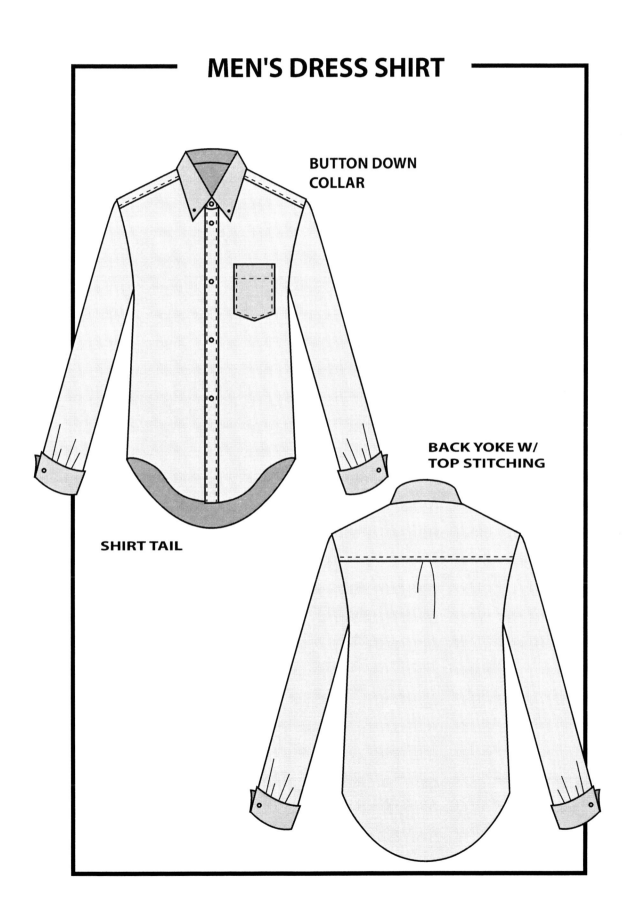

BUTTON DOWN COLLAR

BACK YOKE W/ TOP STITCHING

SHIRT TAIL

LONG SLEEVE
V- NECK

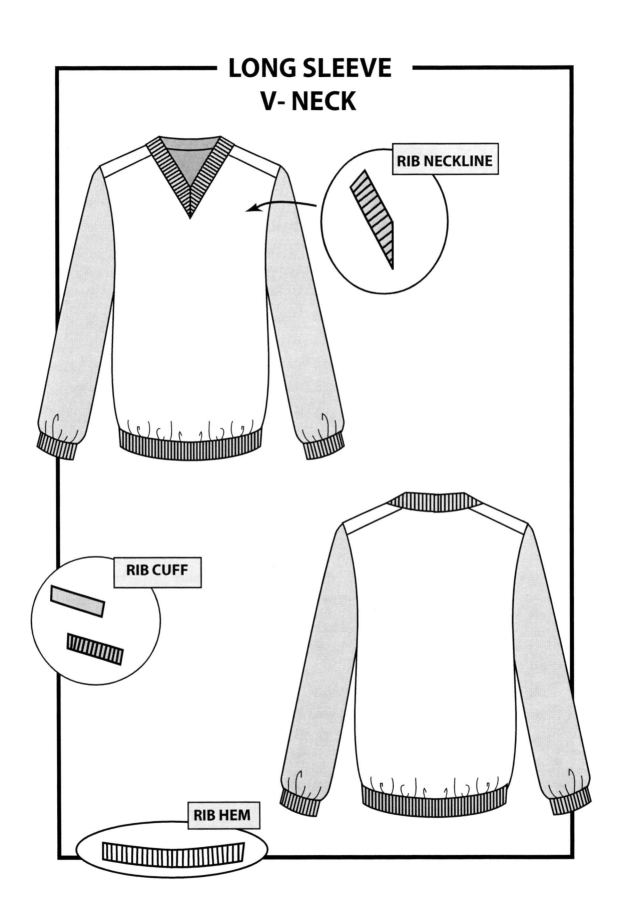

RIB NECKLINE

RIB CUFF

RIB HEM

LONG RAGLAN SLEEVE TOPS

LONG RAGLAN SLEEVE W/ STRIPE CHEST & SLEEVE

RIBBED V- NECKLINE W/ RAGLAN SLEEVES

SEND RIB TO BACK OF SLEEVE *pg 7*

QUILTED VEST

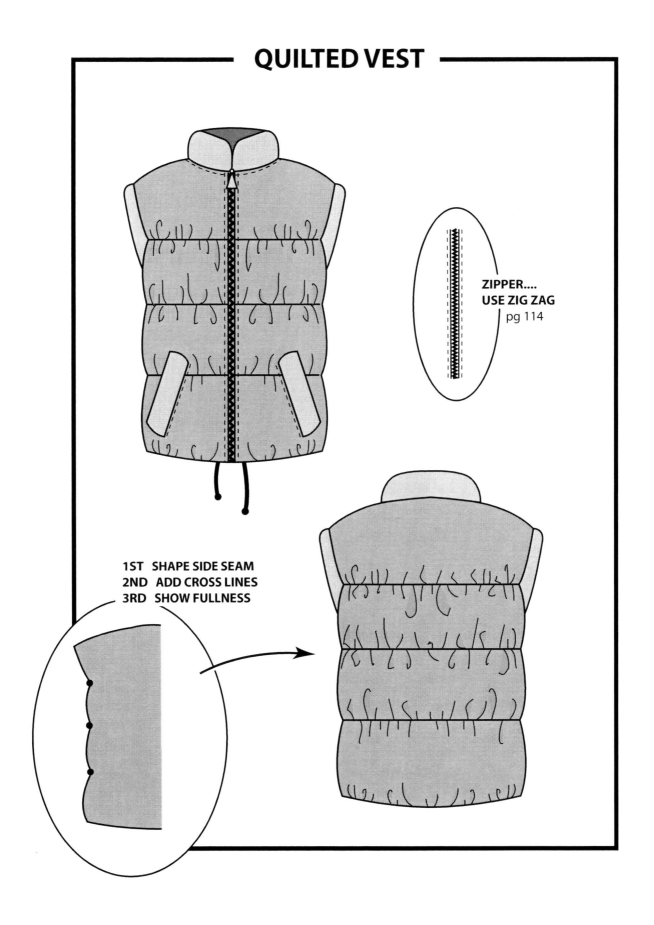

ZIPPER....
USE ZIG ZAG
pg 114

1ST   SHAPE SIDE SEAM
2ND   ADD CROSS LINES
3RD   SHOW FULLNESS

JACKET W/RIB COLLAR
CUFF & HEMLINE

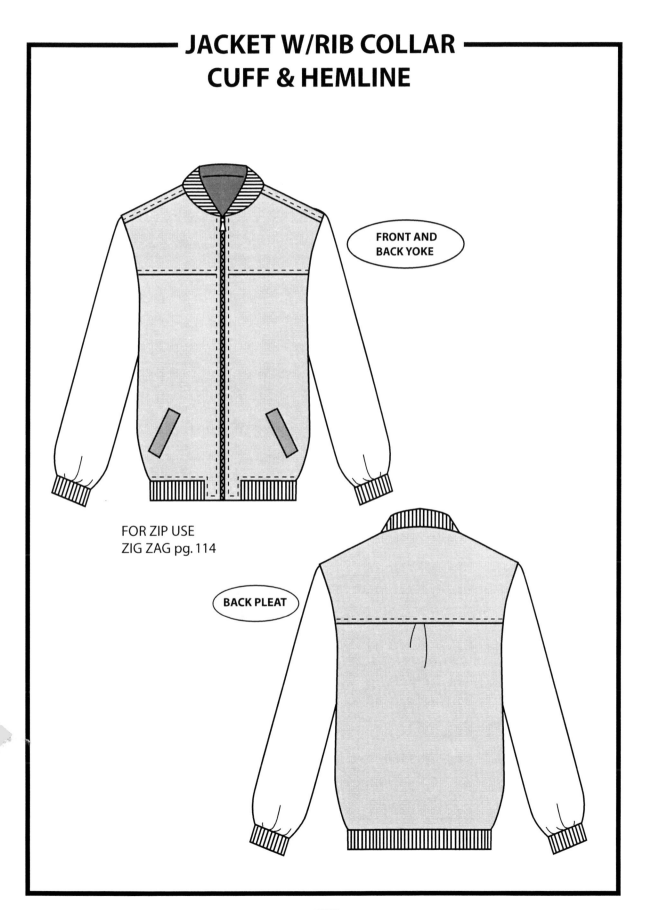

FRONT AND
BACK YOKE

FOR ZIP USE
ZIG ZAG pg. 114

BACK PLEAT

DOUBLE BREASTED JACKET
W/ NOTCH COLLAR

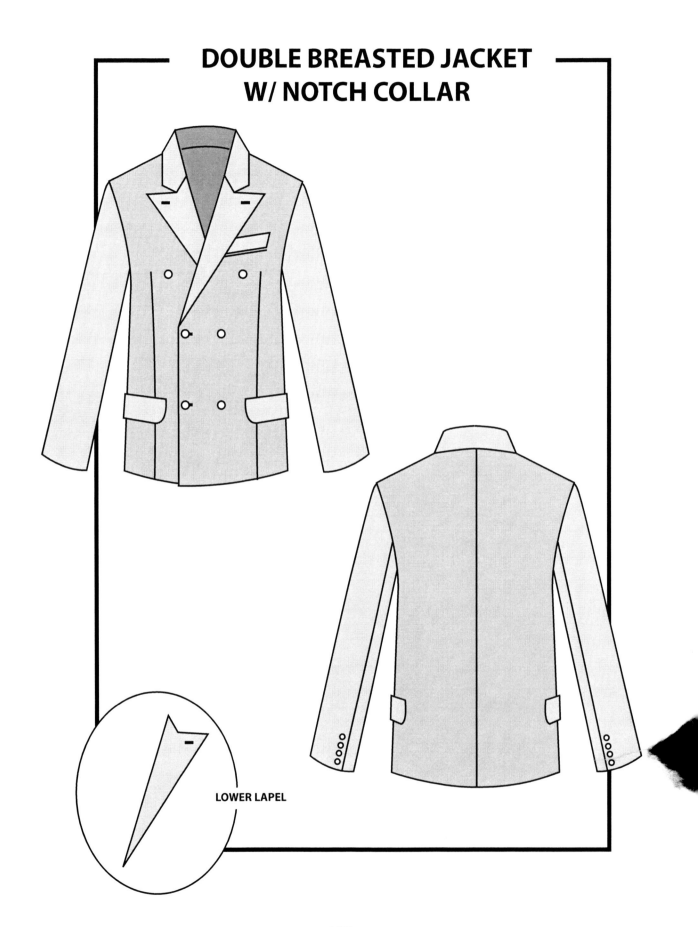

LOWER LAPEL

POLAR HIKING JACKET

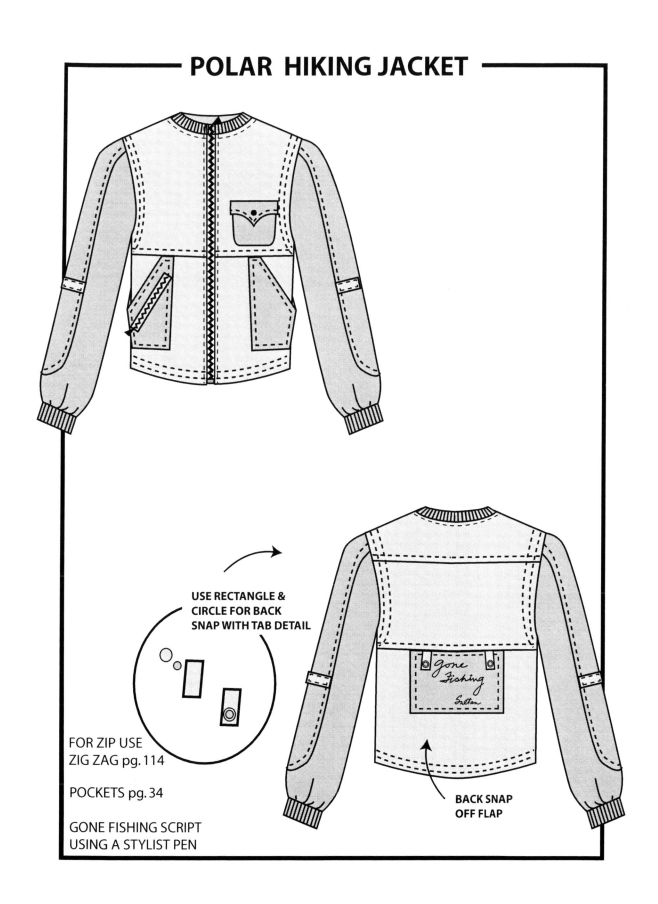

USE RECTANGLE &
CIRCLE FOR BACK
SNAP WITH TAB DETAIL

FOR ZIP USE
ZIG ZAG pg. 114

POCKETS pg. 34

GONE FISHING SCRIPT
USING A STYLIST PEN

BACK SNAP
OFF FLAP

gone
Fishing